EXPLORING THE STEPS OF THE
APOSTLE PAUL IN SPAIN

Explore the forgotten history of Paul's last missionary trip to Spain and Discover Spain's Enormous Influence in the Evolution of Christianity

FERNANDO FIGUEREDO, PhD

Copyright © 2019, by Fernando Figueredo, PhD.

All rights reserved, including the right of reproduction in whole or in part of any form. No part of this book may be reproduced in any manner whatsoever without written permission except in the case of brief quotations in critical articles and reviews.

Manufactured in the United States of America

First Edition

Published by Amazon Kindle Direct Publishing

Title: *Exploring the Steps of the Apostle Paul in Spain*

Cover and interior design by: Adina Cucicov

For information about this book, visit www.historytraveltours.com, or contact info@historytraveltours.com for more information

About the painting on the cover: St. Paul by El Greco (1606): This painting is the famous depiction of the Apostle Paul by the famous Spanish Renaissance artist Doménikos Theotokópoulos, who was born in Crete and was referred to in Spain, and around Europe, as El Greco. The painting can be found in the Museum of El Greco in Toledo, Spain. El Greco is best known for his religious paintings, some of the most famous including St. Paul, The Disrobing of Christ (1577-79) and the Burial of the Count of Orgaz (1587)

No Copyright: The art work on the cover has been identified as being free of known restrictions under copyright law, including all related and neighboring rights. The pictures included throughout the book are being properly sourced in the end notes section of the book.

In dedication to my wife Celi, who supported me through the many paths that kept opening up as my research continued to expand beyond its original scope. At times, after reviewing elements of my research, she would provide insights that allowed me to "connect the dots." She helped me reach the conclusion that there was a very high probability, indeed almost a certainty, that the Apostle Paul had conducted his last missionary trip to Hispania. By discussing my research with her, we both reached a point where we understood Hispania had played one of the most important roles in the evolution of early Christianity, and the protection and defense of the faith through the Middle Ages. It then led the most extensive expansion of the faith in the history of Christianity. Quite honestly, without her insights, I would have never reached the conclusions presented in this book.

~ FERNANDO FIGUEREDO, 2019

TABLE OF CONTENTS

Prologue xi

INTRODUCTION: Establishing the Basis for the Main Premise
Presented in this Book 1

CHAPTER 1: Hispania in Roman Times Provided Fertile Ground
for the Foundation of Early Christian Communities 19

CHAPTER 2: New Testament Writings that Support Paul's High
Priority Missionary Trip to Hispania 33

   A. What does the New Testament say about Paul? Why is he
      referred to as an Apostle? 38
   B. Bible Passages on Paul's Mission to Convert Gentiles
      based on Direction from Jesus 43
   C. Letter to Romans Explains Why Reaching Hispania was
      a High Priority for Paul 46
   D. Acts of the Apostles by Luke: Paul is Jailed and Spends
      the Next Four to Five Years Under Roman Detention 52
   E. Paul must have been set free 55
   F. Paul's Message to Timothy: 2Tim 4:6-8, Paul Implies He
      Has Accomplished Everything He Intended to do 58

CHAPTER 3: Evidence Paul Made the Trip Provided by Three Early
Independent Documents from the First and Second Century 61

   A. Evidence Supported by a Very Important Early Church
      Father: St. Clement, Third Bishop of Rome, His Letter to
      the Corinthians, 96 AD 62

B. The Muratorian Fragment ... 67
   C. Apocryphal Acts of Peter ... 70

CHAPTER 4: The Writings from Six Other Early "Doctors" of the Church ... 75
   A. Saint Athanasius, Bishop of Alexandria between 328 and 373AD ... 77
   B. Saint Cyril, Bishop of Jerusalem from 350 to 386AD[68] ... 79
   C. Saint John Chrysostom, Archbishop of Constantinople from 397 to 407AD ... 80
   D. Saint Jerome [Jeronimo] (Eusebius Sophronius Hieronymus, 347-420AD) ... 82
   E. St. Epiphanius of Salamis, Bishop of Cyprus from 365 to 403 ... 84
   F. St. Theodoret of Cyrus, Bishop of Cyrus 423 to 457 [76] ... 85
   G. Personal Insights derived from the writings of these six early Christian Church Fathers ... 86

CHAPTER 5: Documenting the Strong Oral Tradition of Eastern Orthodox Churches as well as Cities in Spain that Paul Made the Trip ... 89
   A. The Oral Tradition from the Eastern Orthodox Churches ... 92
   B. Oral Traditions from Within Spain that Paul Preached in Hispania ... 94

CHAPTER 6: Highlighting One Contrary Position: Gelasius—1, Bishop of Rome in the Year 496 AD ... 101

CHAPTER 7: The Famous Council of Elvira in Granada, Year 302-304AD: Does It Support the Probability that Paul Planted the Christian Seeds for These Communities? ... 111

CHAPTER 8: In the True Missionary Spirit of Paul, Hispania/Spain's Ultimate Mission: The Recovery, Protection, and Expansion of Christianity ... 127
   A. Growth of Christianity in Hispania by the Visigoths in the VI and VII Century AD ... 135
   B. Islamic Invasion of Hispania ... 137
   C. The Recovery (Re-conquest) of Christian Hispania from the Muslims ... 141

CHAPTER 9: Establishing the Steps of the Apostle Paul in Hispania 157
  A. Establishing the Steps of St. Paul in Hispania/Spain 164
  B. Additional Comments on the Possibility St. James Also Visited Hispania 171
  C. Purpose of this chapter 172

CHAPTER 10: Final Comments and Conclusions 173
  A. Paul Travelled to Hispania 174
  B. Is the Council of Elvira (Granada), which was Enormously Important to Early Christianity, an Indication Paul Founded Christianity in Hispania? 175
  C. Bishop Osio of Cordoba Emerged as One of the Most Important Early Christian Theologians 177
  D. The Critical Role Played by the Early Visigoth Christian Kings in the Recovery of Their Lands from the Muslims Could Have Saved Christianity from Extinction 181
  E. Evangelization of the Americas 181
  F. Final Comments 182

APPENDIX: The Historical Importance of the Region of Al-Andalus in the Evolution of Philosophical Concepts of Islam as well as Judaism 185

End Notes 199
Bibliography 207
About the Author 213

PROLOGUE

God works in mysterious ways. He often puts great opportunities in front of us, but we let them slip away without even noticing those opportunities were there. How many times have you looked back in life and thought to yourself: "If I had only been paying attention?"

I was blessed with such an opportunity and was lucky enough to pay attention in time to realize I had come across several very important findings. Speaking with my wife one day in the summer of 2013, we realized that through informal research I had been conducting since 2008, that I had inadvertently collected a vast amount of information that showed Hispania, as Spain was known in Roman Empire times, had been immensely influential in the evolution of Christianity. Being a Catholic of Cuban heritage, I knew that Spain had a strong Catholic heritage, but I had no Idea that next to Rome, it was probably the most important region in protecting and spreading Christianity around the world.

My research led me through a ten-year journey of discovery that showed that by the year 302 AD, the southern Baetica province of Hispania was a region with one of the highest densities of Christians in all of Christendom. By the year 600 AD, the entire Iberia peninsula was a Christian stronghold under the rule of the Visigoth Christians. This followed the 700-year intense struggle by the Christians to recover what had been their Christian lands after the surprised Muslim invasion of 711 AD. This was a period during which the Christian faithful and their kings slowly and valiantly fought to recover their Christian lands, guided by a very deep faith that the Muslims were never able to eradicate. And they did this without the military help from Popes or from other countries.

Their efforts, together with those of Charles Martell in southern France in the VIII century, in effect, were critical in keeping Christianity from being exterminated. And then, as if salvaging Christianity wasn't enough, beginning at the end of the XV century with Colombus' discovery of the Americas, the kings and missionaries of Hispania led the most important expansion of Christianity in history. They accomplished this impressive expansion with little help from any other country, with the exception of Portugal and its evangelization of most of Brazil. It's actually an intriguing historical fact to put into proper context that the most important expansion of Christianity came from the two countries that had its origins coming from what had been Hispania in the Iberia Peninsula.

The more I studied the ever-increasing historical elements that kept "popping-up" during my research, the more convinced I became that Hispania had been immensely influential in the evolution and expansion of Christianity. In fact, it was hard to find any other region of the world that had the same level of influence on the religion. Rome, as the seat of Christianity with its Papal line going back to Peter as the first Bishop of Rome, was undeniably important as the center of the religion. But my research showed that historians had given Hispania very little credit in the early evolution, defense, protection, and eventual expansion of Christianity.

So, how did this ten-year journey of discovery begin? It began in 2008 when my wife and I stumbled across a very surprising piece of information that showed the Apostle Paul had conducted a missionary trip to Hispania. This surprise finding happened towards the end of the four years I spent working on my doctoral degree at the University of Seville's College of Mass Communication, one of the top ranked faculties of Journalism and Mass Communication in Europe.

It happened quickly. My wife, Celi, in the summer of 2008, had been wanting to visit the small city of Ecija, which has a population of around 40,000 and a rich history going back to Roman times. She had heard about the amazing Roman museum and about its reputation as the City of Towers, in reference to the many church towers in the city. She then organized a long weekend trip for us to visit towns around Seville and decided at the last minute to book one night in Ecija.

When we arrived in Ecija, we found that the churches in the town were having celebrations venerating the Apostle Paul, who we discovered was the Patron Saint of Ecija. At Mass that Sunday, we were intrigued when the priest referred to the oral tradition that Paul had been in Ecija on a missionary trip between the years 64 and 66 AD. I had never heard that the Apostle Paul had been in Spain, although Celi mentioned at the time she had read in the New Testament the references of Paul wanting to go to Spain.

After Mass, we went to speak with the sacristan of the church and he explained that Pope Benedict had just declared a "Holy Year of Jubilee" for Ecija, from June 2008 to June 2009 in honor of Paul's missionary trip there. The sacristan explained the very strong oral tradition that Paul had preached in Ecija in the first century and pledged he would return in the future. That pledge, according to oral tradition, was kept when, in 1436, a well-documented miracle took place in which Paul appeared to a local peasant and told him the people of Ecija needed to return to their Christian ways. We'll provide a more extended explanation of the miracle in Chapter-5, but suffice to say that ever since 1436, there has been an annual celebration and pilgrimage by residents of the towns around Ecija in honor of Paul's missionary trip.

I was so intrigued by this story that it almost felt like I had had a personal encounter with the Apostle Paul. That "encounter," launched a ten-year journey that resulted in publishing this book.

Coincidently, when we returned to our home town of Miami a week later, we confirmed what the sacristan in the Ecija church had told us. Pope Benedict XVI called for celebrating *"The Year of St. Paul"* throughout Catholic churches in the world but had given Ecija a special designation of a "Jubilee Year." It then dawned on me why for Ecija in particular, the Pope had called for this special Year of Jubilee to be celebrated at every church in the town. I became so intrigued with all of these mentions of Paul, that a burning desired erupted in me to further research his trip and the Church's concept behind "jubilee years."

After obtaining my doctoral degree, I then began a much more intense research project on this subject, and after ten years, it has led to the conclusions presented herein. What I didn't realize at the beginning of my research, was that I was coming across a significant amount of information by accident. It was almost as if there was a higher power making sure it was placed in front of me so I would pay attention to it and write about it.

I suddenly began to notice the deep devotion and veneration by the people of Spain to the Virgin Mary, to Jesus Christ, and to the saints. Whether those people went to Mass on Sunday or not, thousands would line up in the streets on special Christian holidays to pay solemn homage while holy images went by carried by church members. Figure-1 shows one of the many Christian processions that take place in small villages or large cities across Spain every year during Holy week, with this particular image showing the city of Seville. Spending Easter week in Spain is an experience that makes you aware of the deep Christian roots that exists in the country. It is no wonder Ernest Hemingway once wrote that every person should spend one Easter Week in Seville sometime during their life.

Fig. 1: One of many inspirational Holy Week processions in Seville, celebrating Christianity.

A remarkable process of discovery started to evolve quickly after I started my research. As a result of looking into the possibility of Paul's missionary trip to Hispania, other critical elements on the importance of Hispania to the evolution of Christianity started to become evident. It seemed that each area of research would lead to the discovery of another important historical element that focused on early Christianity in Hispania.

And the research surrounding that discovery would itself lead to discover another historical element of early Christianity in Hispania. One discovery led to another. It was an amazing process that led me to conclude that Hispania had been one of the most important regions in the world in the evolution of the Christian religion. I began to realize that there was really no other region of the world that had had such an impact in both, the development of Christian beliefs as well as in the expansion of the religion around the world.

My research also led me to realize that Spain's importance had been lost in history. Many of the books and documents I researched gave Rome, Greece and the Asia Minor regions most of the credit for the evolution of Christianity. Hispania, which I now knew played an immensely important role, was hardly ever mentioned. A country that was crucial in preventing the eradication of Christianity by Islamic forces and was later responsible for the most important expansion of the religion throughout the Americas and the Pacific, received little mention in most of the literature I researched.

The intriguing part is that I discovered each of the elements presented in this book by accident. I was not looking for them. The fact that Celi and I arrived in Ecija almost by "coincidence," on the Year of St. Paul, is a good example since that coincidental trip almost didn't happen.

It's important to note here that this phenomenon, of a "coincidental" finding, is a very typical circumstance in research. Researchers often accidentally discover an important element while researching another area of their studies. It happens almost by coincidence. It is then up to the researcher to "connect-the-dots," using those research dots to reach conclusions beyond the original scope of that research.

That is precisely what I have done in this book. I have presented a number of historical elements that when "connected" allow you to reach the conclusion that Spain had an enormous influence in the evolution of Christianity, and in particular, in the development of early Christian beliefs and norms.

An important proof-point that I'll mention here but expand considerably in Chapter-7 is that by the year 302 AD, Christians in the Roman province of Hispania established and published the first documented set of norms for Christians to live their lives. This happened at the Council of Iliberis (Granada, Spain), which has been well-documented by the Church as the first published set of norms and beliefs in Church history. Iliberis was a town in the Roman Province of Baetica, today's Andalucía. This Province has been documented as having had one of the highest numbers of Christian communities in early Christianity.

So then, why was Christianity so well-established in the Baetica region by the year 300 AD, and why did so many other critical elements in the early evolution of Christianity originate in Hispania?

The obvious answer is that a highly passionate missionary had to be the catalyst to plant such ardent religious belief in the people of Hispania. The only one with documented historical references from early Christianity to support a presence in Hispania was the Apostle Paul himself, as will be explained in the book.

As I continued to dig deeper into this subject matter, I began to realize that the influence of Spain in the evolution and expansion of Christianity didn't stop in the early years of Christianity. In fact, it had an even bigger influence throughout the Middle-Ages with the re-conquest and recovery of Christian territories from the Muslims, and later with the evangelization of the Americas.

Again, I asked myself, why has Spain not been given its rightful place by biblical historians on its importance in the evolution of Christianity? The answers to these questions and the insights gleamed from the research are presented in this book. Those answers led a Bishop from a major city in Spain that I interviewed, Archbishop Jaume Pujol of the Archdiocese of Tarragona (one hour south of Barcelona) to make an interesting statement: "It's noteworthy to see that someone from outside of Spain conducted this research and 'connected the dots.'"

Archbishop Pujol's comments and support became an early inspiration for the research I was conducting. Equally important in my early research was Father Armand Puig, who at the time was the Dean of the Theological Faculty of Catalunya, based in Barcelona. Fr. Puig provided several important insights into that last missionary trip of Paul to Hispania. He is a highly distinguished and respected biblical historian who had an important role in the 2008 conference held in Tarragona on the Apostle Paul's missionary trip to Tarragona. At this conference, the 31 biblical historians, theologians and archeologists, concluded that Paul travelled to Hispania, entering through Tarraco, todays Tarragona.

In addition to Archbishop Pujol and Fr. Puig, there were a number of other very important biblical historians who would unexpectedly be referred to my attention.

Fig. 2: Left-Andreu Muñoz, Director-Biblical Museum Tarragona Right: Fr. Armand Puig, Dean-Theological Faculty of Catalunya

Two of those were Dr. Andreu Muñoz, Director of the Biblical Museum of Tarragona, and Marisa Jimenez, Director of the Seminari of Tarragona.

They provided insights and information on the Apostle Paul's highly probable missionary trip to Hispania, very likely landing in Tarragona. They also provided information on the history of early Christians in Hispania, especially in the then Roman Province of Tarraconensis.

I would be remised if I didn't also mention two additional biblical historians who provided a significant amount of information at the early stage of my research on the evolution of Christianity in Hispania. The first is Father Jaime Sancho from the Archdiocese of Valencia and the second is Father Manuel Martin Riego of the Archdiocese of Seville.

Fig. 3: Fr. Jaime Sancho—Cathedral of Valencia

As of the publishing of this book, Fr. Jaime was the Canonical responsible for the Cathedral of Valencia as well as the Chapel of the Holy Chalice of the Last Supper. He provided an invaluable amount of information on how the Holy Chalice arrived in Hispania in the year 258, and later to the Cathedral in Valencia. The story of the Holy Chalice of Valencia has been covered by National Geographic, with the conclusion that the only Church around the world that could claim to hold the Chalice of the Last Supper is the one in Valencia.

Its history supports the arguments that Hispania was a safer place during the first three centuries for Christians and their relics. As such, many biblical historians believe it is evidence that for so many Christian communities to have been established in Hispania by the year 300, a very significant missionary effort had to have started by the second half of the first century. That missionary effort many now believe would have been led by the Apostle Paul around the years 64-66.

Fr. Manuel for his part as the Director and Editor of the Center for Theological Studies of Seville, provided detailed information on Christian communities in the first three centuries in the Baetica Province, today's Community of Andalucía. His work as the Director has been invaluable in the documentation and preservation of important historical information on the Church in the community of Andalucía.

Fig. 4: Fr. Manuel Martin Riego, Director- Seville Center for Theological Studies

Fr. Manuel's insights and counsel on the evolution of Christian communities in what was then the Baetica Province of the Roman Empire also led me to conclude there was a strong possibility Paul preached in this region of Hispania.

There were many other biblical historians, archeologists and religious professors who participated in my research and provided additional information presented in this book. One in particular I would like to thank is historian and archeologist, Dr. Purificación (Puri) Ubric Rabaneda from the University of Granada, for her support and important insights on the Council of Elvira and early Christians in Hispania. The other historians are included in the bibliography section and are referenced throughout the book. The ones specifically mentioned above were critical for the early inspiration they provided and the encouragement to take on this very laborious and arduous task of compiling and making sense of so much information.

In this regard, it's been hard to find Christian historians outside of Spain that have undertaken the task to decisively conclude that Spain was so vitally important in the evolution of Christianity. There have certainly been historians that have written about Christianity in Spain and about the important role of the Church in Spain.

Hardly anyone, however, has connected the critical roles Hispania/Spain played in the various periods since the beginning of Christianity to then make a definitive statement about the immense influence Spain had in its evolution. For sure, I have not seen in all the research I have conducted anyone position Spain as perhaps having as much influence as Rome when you combine all the elements mentioned in the book: the early evolution of rules on how Christians should conduct their lives, the protection of Christianity through the recovery of their Christian lands invaded by the Muslims, the support and protection of the Pope as the line of Christianity emanating from Peter, and the most important expansion of the religion through the evangelization of the Americas.

I've been blessed, perhaps by the hand of the Holy Spirit, to have paid attention to all the information that was placed in front of me that allowed me to develop such conclusions. When we combine them all, you can clearly see that Spain has had one of the most important roles in the growth of Christianity, and certainly of Catholicism.

I therefore want to thank the many church leaders, Christian scholars, historians and archeologists, in Spain, in the Vatican and in Miami, where I reside, that have collaborated and provided information for this work. One from Miami that I would like to highlight for his continued encouragement is Father Ernesto Fernandez Travieso, Jesuit Priest and professor at Belen Jesuit school. Fr. Ernesto understood early on that this book could be a very important work that needed to be published and disseminated.

And from an academician perspective, I would like to express my personal thanks to the Chair of my doctoral dissertation at the University of Seville, Dr. Juan Luis Manfredi. Dr. Manfredi provided invaluable insights for my dissertation, and because of his deep devotion to Christianity, in effect facilitated the exploration of this topic following my years of studies at the University of Seville.

Most important of all, as I mentioned in the dedication of this book, I specifically want to thank my wife, Celi, who has been a strong supporter and partner through the very intense and arduous task of writing and editing this book. She was the first to notice the probable presence of Paul in Hispania, and that was the spark that lit the fire under me to launch this research project of ten years. Her insights and guidance along the way provided a very significant level of input into the final edition of this book, and for that, I will always be grateful.

~ FERNANDO FIGUEREDO, PH.D.
Founder—History Travel Tours
Miami—Sevilla
2019

Introduction

ESTABLISHING THE BASIS FOR THE MAIN PREMISE PRESENTED IN THIS BOOK

Since the beginning of Christianity, Hispania, as Spain was known in Roman Empire times, has played a crucial role in the evolution and subsequent growth of the religion. And yet, most biblical historians have focused their research on Rome, Asia Minor, and other Christian regions. As a result, few biblical historians outside of Spain have highlighted throughout the centuries the immense positive influence Spain has had in the initial evolution and later expansion of Christianity.

I've often been puzzled by this fact. My research over the past ten years has convinced me that Hispania had been vitally important to the survival, protection and propagation of Christianity. In fact, during the first 300 years of Christianity, Christian communities in Hispania grew and solidified to become among the most important and best organized in early Christendom, but this fact is scarcely mentioned in biblical-historical books outside of Spain.

Fig. 5: Map of early Christianity—Black represents by the year 300 AD[1]

As Fig. 5 shows, it's been well-documented by Church historians that by the year 300 AD the Iberia Peninsula, which was named the region of Hispania by the Romans, had a large presence of Christian communities. This was especially true in the Baetica Province of Hispania, today's Community of Andalucía in Spain, which at the time had one of the largest population densities in the Roman Empire.

If we go back to the time of Christ, the region of Hispania had been divided into three Roman provinces: Tarraconensis, Lusitania and Baetica. Governors of these provinces were consumed with the tasks of gathering and providing the enormous demands for agricultural, food, and mining products back to the Roman Empire. As a result, their focus on persecuting Christians was not as brutal as that of the Roman Emperors or of governors in other regions. Some historians have actually hypothesized that by the end of the third century, the Baetica province could have had the highest density of Christians[2] when compared to other Christian regions of early Christianity.

As we will present in this book, during the first three centuries after Christ, the tenets and beliefs of what it meant to be a Christian developed to an advanced level in the region of Hispania, especially in the Baetica province. That's where the first Christian Council in Church history was held in which rules and canons for how Christians should lead their daily lives were documented and published for the first time. It became known as the Council of Elvira, and it was held in the year 302/304 AD. Chapter-7 of this book covers the Council of Elvira in more detail.

It's been challenging for biblical historians to find clear evidence of how Christianity initially reached Hispania. No one knows for sure who was responsible for "planting the seeds" of the religion there. In recent years, this issue has been studied by an increasing number of biblical historians. Of special interest by these historians has been to determine why there was such rapid and extensive growth of Christian communities throughout Hispania in those first three centuries of the religion, especially in its southern province of Baetica.

Many have suggested that this growth required the intense missionary efforts by one of Jesus' closest apostles. A few researchers in the past fifty years have advanced the theory that the Apostle Paul could have been responsible for being the first to preach the Word of Christ in Hispania.[3] I am also presenting the same premise in this book, citing a number of vitally important historical documents that these other researchers also previously presented. However, I have compiled and presented what I believe to be the most complete set of such documents, and at the same time, adding additional research findings that I have uncovered as evidence. Together, they create a very strong and credible set of historical documents that provide evidence that points to Paul as the source for planting the seeds of Christianity in Hispania.

Paul had an extensive record of convincing new converts into the religion and of creating a high level of fervor in those individuals, leaving detailed guidelines on how Christians should lead their lives.

When you look at the characteristics of the many Christian communities in Hispania, especially at the canons that came out of the Council of Elvira, Paul's influence appears to be all over them. If you further combine these characteristics with the historical evidence being presented in this book, we can easily reach the conclusion that he absolutely could have been the force to set in motion the rapid growth of Christianity in Hispania.

We cannot discount, however, another very strong Spanish tradition that points to the Apostle James the Greater as the one responsible for planting the seeds of Christianity in Hispania. This tradition began in the ninth century and was reinforced with additional documentation towards the end of the Middle Ages. But many biblical historians have concluded that the tradition of St. James (SanTiago) having preached throughout the region of Galicia in northern Hispania is very doubtful. Galicia is where tradition says is the burial place of Santiago after his bones were transferred to Hispania by his disciples following his execution in the year 40 AD. This is a possibility explained in various section of the book, although the evidence is very slim.

That said, there is much more ancient documentation from the first four centuries that Paul actually made a missionary trip to Hispania. We will delve into this subject in more detail in chapter-2 through chapter-6 of the book.

At this point we need to make special mention of the fact that there were many martyrs in Hispania that gave up their lives during the early years of Christianity. Tarraco, which was the capital of the Province of Tarraconensis and how today's Tarragona was known in Roman times, was among the first to have documented cases of martyrdom. Those martyrs included St. Fructuoso, Bishop of Tarraco, and his deacons, Eulogio and Augurio. All three were executed in 259 AD for not renouncing their faith. In fact, the Archdioceses in Catalunya (Spain) have established Tarragona as "Ground Zero" (Kilometro Zero), for where Christianity started in Hispania.[4]

Those early martyrs gave up their lives as a result of several persecutions launched by Roman emperors during the second, third and early fourth centuries. Even though these persecutions were not as brutal in Hispania as in other parts of the Empire, there were still a number of martyrs in Hispania that were willing to die for their Christian faith.

The deep faith that was engraved into people's hearts, so deep that they were willing to die for, must have been planted by the energy and charisma of someone like St. Paul. It's hard to argue, as some have done, that this deep devotion evolved from the simple migration of Christians from Rome and other regions. If this was the case, who would have established those first communities and their first bishops? Who would have given the authority to such an independent community of Christians who felt by the third century they had the authority to set rules for how Christians should lead their lives? And they did it without checking with any other Christian authority, whether from Rome, the northern Africa churches, or anywhere else?

This only makes sense if the first Christian communities in Hispania had been established by a very "high" Christian authority figure who was blessed with an enormous talent for conversions. And as some historians have concluded, and I concur, it had to have been done towards the second half of the first century for Christianity to have expanded to so many other Christian communities by the third century.

Whoever that high Christian authority figure was, whether an individual or several disciples, they must have left those early bishops with the charge to continue to expand Christianity in the peninsula. When you consider that those early communities independently developed very detailed guidelines on how to lead their Christian lives, as exhibited by the canons of the Council of Elvira, they clearly felt they had the independent "authority" within Christianity to do so.

It makes little sense that without having the direct line back to someone with a very high level of authority, that the 19 Christian bishops in the Council of Elvira would have felt they had the authority to establish such strict canons without getting approval from another Christian authority.

This deep devotion and the well-developed Christian guidelines must have had as the original source someone with the passion, intense focus and clear authority to have initiated it all.

The research I have conducted has led me to conclude that Paul was indeed that original source. This research has been done in collaboration and support from biblical historians, church leaders and archeologists in Spain. As a result, Paul's missionary trip established what would become one of the most important regions of the world in relation to the evolution, future protection, and expansion of Christianity.

An intriguing phenomenon started to evolve as I continued my research on Paul having been in Hispania. The deeper I dug into early Christianity in Hispania, other critical historical elements kept popping up that pointed to Hispania as a safer place for early Christians to live and practice their faith. Hispania's vital importance to early Christianity began to become evident.

These elements indicated Hispania had one of the most important roles in the evolution of Christianity. To my surprise, however, it also had an important influence on Jewish and Islamic tenets, with philosophers from both religions having developed ideological concepts that are still in effect today.

I discovered that there had been Jewish settlements in the southern region of Hispania since before the Roman occupation, and that early Christian communities were established in the same general vicinity as those settlements. As enumerated in the next page, one discovery led to another, and that has become the theme of this book: **Exploring the Steps of the Apostle Paul in Spain,** and in the process, I discovered the importance Spain had in the evolution of Christianity. There were many discoveries, but the more important ones, with one leading to the next, included:

1) Paul made the trip to Hispania between the years 64-66; by the end of 1st century there were Christian communities already established in Hispania, leading to the premise that an intense missionary effort had started years before. My research findings and conclusions pointed to that missionary effort having been launched by the Apostle Paul.
2) That research led to the discovery that the first council in Church history where rules were set for how Christians should run their lives, was held in Hispania at the Council of Elvira in the year 302, in what is today Granada.
3) This led to the discovery that Bishop Osio of Cordoba, who presided over the Council of Elvira, was chosen by Emperor Constantine to preside over the most important council in Church history, the Council of Nicaea in the year 325.
4) This led to the discovery, or perhaps my "realization" is a better way to describe it, that Constantine must have felt Osio was one of the most important leaders of Christianity throughout the Roman Empire. The fact Constantine chose a Bishop from Hispania, and not the Bishop of Rome, or of Jerusalem, or any other bishop, to preside over an immensely important Council for Christianity, implies Hispania had to have been a critically important Christian region. Many priests with whom I have spoken, and even biblical historians, had any idea this was the case.
5) My studies then led me to the awareness that the Christian Kings & people of Hispania were critically important in protecting Christianity. They also led the largest expansion of Christianity with the evangelization of the Americas.

As I continued to research these elements, I started to become aware that there were two additional critical points that needed to be added to the discussion.

The first is that although it took seven centuries, it was the commitment to Christianity by the people and kings of Hispania that led to the recovery of their Christian lands lost to the Muslim invaders in the year 711. By stopping the continued growth of Islam into western Europe, the Christian people of Hispania avoided the potential eradication of Christianity, since those Islamic forces would have likely continued east and connected with the middle eastern Islamic forces.

The people of Hispania were therefore a major force in protecting Christianity in its early years.

The second point is that immediately after they recovered their lost Christian territories, the Kings and missionaries from what used to be Hispania—mostly Spain, with Portugal included—launched the most important expansion in the history of Christianity by evangelizing the Americas. These last two major accomplishments, recovering their Christian lands during the Middle Ages and expanding Christianity to the Americas, were done by the people of Hispania with little help from Rome or any other country.

The only conclusion I could reach when I "connected-the-dots" from this significant amount of research, was that Hispania had an enormous impact in the evolution, protection and expansion of Christianity. Together with Rome, it played perhaps the most important role in Christendom in its early evolution and subsequent expansion.

As explained by biblical historian Jorge Rodriguez, President of the Sindonology Center of Spain, "There is no doubt that the historical mission of Spain was the global spread of Christianity."[5]

That's why it is so important to ask the question: Who planted the seeds for this amazing and passionate commitment to Christianity? It is the premise of this book, based on the evidence presented, that it was the Apostle Paul, with the guidance of the Holy Spirit, who planted those seeds. In doing so, he established a firm base for the eventual growth throughout the Iberian Peninsula.

This book will therefore cover a number of elements to support these conclusions. The fact that I connect a number of historical and biblical elements to document Paul's missionary trip to Spain, and then Spain to the evolution and expansion of Christianity, is the reason why this book has been written. Few historians have ever made all of these historical connections and combined them into one book that makes this definitive conclusion.

In order to present the arguments in the book in a logical manner, I have divided the book into chapters that independently address each of the main points presented.

Chapter 1: Paul Was Aware that Hispania in Roman Times Provided Fertile Ground for the Foundation of Early Christian Communities. It is critical to begin by establishing the premise that Paul was aware Hispania had become fertile ground for the establishment of Christianity. Few people today realize that Hispania was vitally important to the Roman Empire during the time of Christ. It included three well established Imperial Provinces: Tarraconensis, Lusitania, and Baetica, from which large amounts of minerals, agriculture, and industrial products were exported to the Roman capital every day[6]. There is significant documentation that Jewish communities existed throughout the southern Baetica Province, which is an important point since Paul, who was Jewish, often visited Jewish communities first, and immediately after, continued to preach to Gentiles. This chapter will lay the foundation for understanding the importance of Hispania as a Roman region in having favorable conditions, or as we mention here, being "fertile ground" for the spread of Christianity.

Chapter 2: New Testament Writings that Support Paul's High Priority Missionary Trip to Hispania. In his letter to the Romans (Chapter 15) Paul is very clear in stating that he would visit the Church members in Rome while *"passing"* on his way to Hispania. Rome was not his priority, it was Hispania. The Evangelist Luke provides tantalizing information in his Acts of the Apostles to suggest Paul was freed after his two years in Roman house-arrest. This would have given Paul the freedom to accomplish his high-priority trip. It's important to also note that in several other New Testament passages, Paul makes it clear Jesus had assigned him to focus his mission on the pagan "gentiles." In this chapter, I make the important historical observation that, outside of Rome and its surrounding areas in Italy, Hispania had one of the largest populations of gentiles in the Roman Empire. Finally, one other biblical passage just before he was about to be executed, Paul writes the second letter to his beloved disciple, Timothy. In this letter Paul declares he had "finish the race," implying he had been able to accomplish everything he wanted. Given that Timothy knew Hispania was a high priority to Paul, the clear implication is that he was able to accomplish the trip. This chapter goes into specific detail covering these New Testament passages and their implications.

Chapter 3: Evidence that Paul Made the Trip Provided by Three Early Independent Documents from the First and Second Century: a) Letter from Clement, Bishop of Rome, b) the Muratorian Fragment, c) The Apocryphal Gospel of Peter.
Perhaps the most important piece of evidence that Paul made the trip to Hispania is that Clement-I, the third Bishop of Rome, wrote in the year 96 AD a letter to the Corinthians in which he directly references Paul's missionary trip to Hispania.

Many biblical historians have incredibly discounted Clement's letter, even though Clement must have been very familiar with Paul and his travels. They claim that Clement was confusing Paul's "intention" to travel there as opposed to giving him the credit for actually confirming Paul's trip. But there are two other very important documents from the second century that also give credence to Paul having traveled to Hispania: The Muratorian Fragment and the Apocryphal Gospel of Peter. All three of these documents will be covered in detail in Chapter-3, adding to the evidence that exists of Paul having made the trip.

Chapter 4: Evidence from The Writings of Six Early Doctors of the Church that Paul Made the Trip, all of Whom Were Biblical Historians. As if the material presented in the last two chapters is not enough to prove Paul made the trip to Hispania, we follow with the writings of six early saints who have been designated as "Doctors of the Church" for their writings and insights of Christianity. These writings, all of which took place within the first five centuries, together with the documentation presented in the previous chapters, provide a picture that the early church of the first 500 years had a clear understanding that Paul made his high-priority trip to Hispania.

Chapter 5: Documenting the Strong Oral Tradition of the Eastern Orthodox Churches as well as the Tradition in the Various Cities of Spain Documenting Paul Made the Trip. A very close friend of mine who became a priest many years ago in the Eastern Antiochian Orthodox Christian Church explained to me one day that in the Eastern Orthodox churches the missionary trip of Paul to Hispania is taken as a fact. This was a crucial revelation to me. That the churches that had the closest relationship to Paul, and who must have had detailed knowledge of Paul's travels, considered it a fact Paul traveled to Hispania on a missionary trip, had to be given the fullest acknowledgment in my research. Keep in mind Paul had founded many of these Eastern churches, so since early Christianity they must have been aware of Paul's travels.

Chapter 6: Highlighting One Contrary Position: Gelasius—1, Bishop of Rome in the Year 496, Wrote that Paul was not Able to Make the Trip to Hispania. Historians who over the years have argued that Paul did not make the trip always mention a passage made in the year 496 by Gelasius-I, Bishop of Rome. In one of his encyclicals, Gelasius mentions that even though Paul had a very high priority for going to Hispania, even promising he would make the trip, he was never able to make it due to circumstances coming from above, from a higher power. Because this assertion from Gelasius makes little sense in the face of so much evidence that implies Paul did make the trip, I have dug deep into why Gelasius would make such a declaration. What I have found is an intriguing twist of controversial circumstances taking place at the time Gelasius wrote this passage that could explain why he made such an assertion. In Chapter-6 we cover this point to try to shed light into why he might have made such a controversial statement in view that the common belief of the fifth century Christian community was that Paul made the trip to Hispania.

Chapter 7: The Famous Council of Elvira in Granada, Year 302-304AD: Does it Support the Probability that Paul Planted the Christian Seeds for These Communities? Between the years 300/305AD, the first documented Christian Council in Church archives where norms were written down on how Christians should live their lives, took place at the Council of Elvira. The exact year is not known but many historians believe it happened more exactly between the years 302 and 304 AD. There were 19 bishops and 37 Christian communities present, all of them from Hispania. Elvira was the mountain range in which the Roman city of Iliberis was located. Today this is the city of Granada. There were a number of important norms and rules for Christians to follow that came out of this Council that give a tempting comparison to how Paul would provide important rules to follow for the communities he founded. These norms and rules had to have been grounded in a very high Christian authority years before; that is, the individual or disciples who founded these communities had to possess a very high level of authority in Christianity for these norms to have been established so definitive. In fact, many of these rules were later discussed in the Council of Nicaea (325 AD), considered the most important Council in Church history. This is the reason why the Council of Elvira, which preceded Nicaea, was so important. One of the leaders in the Council of Elvira was the famous Bishop Osio of Cordoba, who was later chosen to preside over the Council of Nicaea, becoming one of the most important leaders in early Christian history. Osio must have felt he had the moral and Christian authority, passed down to him from a previous high Christian authority, to have driven the discussion in the Council of Nicaea. Who could that Christian authority be? One obvious conclusion is the Apostle Paul himself, as we confirm in this book.

Chapter 8: In the True Missionary Spirit of Paul, the Ultimate Mission of Hispania/Spain Turned Out to be The Recovery, Protection, and Expansion of Christianity. As I continued my research, it became obvious that the Impact of the Christian Kings and people of Hispania in recovering, protecting and expanding Christianity could not be matched by any other region in the world. The rapid Muslim invasion in 711 AD of what was Christian Visigoths' territory took only ten years to turn most of what was Christian Hispania into the Islamic emirate of Al-Andalus. An impressive historical fact is the story of how a small number of Visigoth Christians who had escaped and lived in a small region of the northern Pyrenees Mountains known as Asturias, never gave up in recovering their Christian lands. In a true example of the "fearless grit" planted by Paul, they were able to defeat a major Muslim army in 722 AD that was trying to exterminate them. That victory began the slow recovery of the Christian lands of Hispania. Eventually, after 700 years and the unification of the Kingdoms of Castilla and Aragon, the last Islamic kingdom of Granada was returned to Christianity in 1492. That led to the most intensive expansion of Christianity in its history. Almost as if driven by the missionary zeal of the Apostle Paul, the Kings and Queens of Spain sponsored missionary priests sent to the newly discovered lands to Christianize its people. These missionary priests protected, and in a number of documented cases, gave up their lives, protecting the native people. My research led me to the conclusion that an important portion of this book needed to be dedicated to the commitment to Christianity by the people and kings of these kingdoms. If not for them, Christianity could have been completely eradicated, and western Europe could have easily become an Islamic Caliphate, eventually connected with the eastern Islamic forces.

Chapter 9: Establishing the Steps of St. Paul in Hispania. Given the preponderance of evidence in favor of Paul having made the trip, the conclusion I have reached is that Paul did in fact go to Hispania, almost certainly arriving in Tarraco, the Imperial capital of the Tarraconensis Province. Is it possible, therefore, to establish where precisely Paul preached while he was in Tarraco and other regions of Hispania? In this chapter I provide evidence of the places he could have preached while in Hispania, especially in Tarraco, where there is a very high level of certainty that this is where he entered Hispania. Soon after he landed in Tarraco, he would have visited the small local Jewish community that existed at that time and would have surely been given permission to speak to its members. He would then move to the other public places where Romans were accustomed to having public speakers address passersby. This would have been the local government forum, and possibly the Circus which was under construction at the time. I have obtained maps from the period of time that Paul would have preached there to trace his steps in Hispania.

Chapter 10: Final Comments and Conclusions. Finally, with all the research material and documentation being presented herein, it's important to provide a summary of how this information led to the conclusions presented. Although we've been careful to document all the points raised in this book, we do not pretend that the material included represents an all-inclusive literature review since there are thousands of books and research reports on Paul's travels and of Christianity in Spain. Nonetheless, the work presented herein is completely backed by research findings from some of the most distinguished biblical historians on the Apostle Paul, university professors, and church leaders. The work presented herein also includes personal interviews with highly respected biblical historians for their input on well-documented archival materials from early church history. This has been done with the intention of positioning this book as an important historical document focused on the evolution of Christianity in Hispania. It should be disseminated and discussed by those interested in religious studies, especially as it pertains to the early growth of Christianity.

I could not complete this book, however, without dedicating a significant section to the fact there were highly distinguished philosophers and religion leaders from both Judaism as well as Islam that came from the region of Hispania. I've therefore added an Appendix to the book to provide a short summary of the presence of leaders from these religions in Appendix A. It was important to add such an appendix since throughout the book there are numerous mentions of how the tenets of both of these religions were discussed and advanced in Hispania during the over 700 years presence of Islam in the peninsula.

The fact is that my research on the early evolution of Christianity in Spain led me to a unique set of insights, and it became clear that over the centuries the region of Hispania became a hotbed for the debate and analysis of religious philosophical concepts. Beyond Christianity, I was astonished to find that several important religious philosophers that influenced the philosophical interpretations of the Torah for Jews and the Quran for Muslims came from this region. In fact, as it relates to the Muslim presence, "The Golden Age of Islam" is a term often used when referring to the Caliphate of Cordoba for the period between the X and XII centuries. There were major advancements during this period, not only in religion but also in the sciences, mathematics, arts and culture. The point we make in the appendix is that Hispania was a special place, with a special energy, that allowed for the evolution of religious and philosophical concepts that later had an impact on all three Abrahamic religions.

The material presented in this book should be considered as "work-in-progress" given that historians and archeologists continue to make findings that attest to the importance of Spain's influence in the evolution of Christianity. This influence continues to this day. A great example is the amazing work of the deeply faithful Antoni Gaudi and his Holy Family Basilica (Basilica de la Sagrada Familia) in Barcelona, begun in 1866 and continues today. It has become one of the most visited Christian sites in the world, which has also gained global tourism attention for its phenomenal advances in architectural and structural elements. Through its monumental architectural features, Gaudi has successfully highlighted important elements of the Bible as well as the importance of God and nature. In doing so, he has positioned this Basilica in Spain as a living testimony of the Bible, thereby expanding Christianity to tourists from all over the world through its magnificence.

Another example is that a number of recent research reports have pointed to the high probability that the Chalice in display in the Cathedral of Valencia is the Chalice of the Last Supper used by Jesus Christ. Even the prestigious National Geographic researchers have come to the same conclusion. Obviously, it is impossible to say definitively that this chalice is the one used in the Last Supper. However, it's amazing history and all the surrounding evidence points to this being the only chalice from the various places around the world that claim to have such a chalice, that could possibly be the Chalice of the Last Supper. I have also conducted my own research and came to the same conclusion.

Yet another example includes the findings 30 years ago, and recently reconfirmed, of the validity of the Oviedo Sudarium (Sudario de Oviedo). These findings indicate that the blood stains in the Sudarium, which has been hypothesized to have covered the face of Jesus after his burial, are aligned identically with the facial blood stains found on the Shroud of Christ in Turin, Italy. Medical researchers had already concluded 30 years ago that the stains in the Sudarium were consistent with the blood stains of someone who had been crucified. Recent findings, however, provide additional elements of validity in that these blood stains, as well as the blood-type, have now been found to match the stains and blood-type of the individual on the Shroud. Both cloths have now been shown to have the same AB blood type, an immensely important finding since only 4% of the population have this type of blood, and they are mostly from the Middle East. Together, 21 different forensic elements have been found to match both cloths. The conclusion reached by many forensic scientists is that, whether or not the two cloths were used to cover Jesus Christ, they were both used to cover the same individual close to two thousand years ago.

These findings allow us to conclude that early Christians considered Hispania an important place to protect relics. This conclusion adds to the validity of one of the main premises of this book, that Hispania was of critical importance in the early evolution of Christianity. These and many other important relics were hidden in Hispania to avoid being destroyed by Roman persecutions and later by persecutions from Muslims. If we consider that the evidence surrounding these relics reaching Hispania is extremely convincing, then the fact they have been found there to avoid being destroyed confirms this premise.

Combining the personal testimony of many other church leaders and church historians with the independent research I have conducted, the two main premises being presented in this book have been validated, that:

1) Paul conducted a missionary trip to Hispania and planted the seeds of Christianity there, and,
2) Hispania/Spain had an immense influence in the evolution, protection, and expansion of Christianity.

This book was written in an attempt to capture all of the information presented herein into one publication, and to then let the readers develop their own conclusions. I hope readers also agree with the conclusions reached and that the information is interesting and compelling. It hopefully will help them expand their knowledge and understanding of the early evolution of Christianity and of the historical importance of Spain in the evolution of Christianity.

CHAPTER 1

HISPANIA IN ROMAN TIMES PROVIDED FERTILE GROUND FOR THE FOUNDATION OF EARLY CHRISTIAN COMMUNITIES

One of the most important insights we're presenting in this book is that in the region of Hispania, as Spain was known during Roman times, Christianity grew and flourished in the early years to become one of the largest Christian regions in the world. This is evident since we know for sure that the first Christian Council in Church history, where they first published the rules and norms of how Christians should lead their lives, was held in the Roman town of Iliberis, today's Granada.

This Council became known as the Council of Elvira. Elvira was the mountain range surrounding the town of Iliberis. Although the exact year is not known, most historians agree it took place between 302-304 AD. This was almost a quarter of a century prior to the famous Council of Nicaea of 325 AD, convened by Emperor Constantine. It is therefore important at this early stage of the book to place Hispania in the proper historical and geographical context for its early importance in the development of Christian norms and beliefs.

Fig. 6: Map shows Hispania at the time of Paul. Roman ships first stopped in Tarraco, conduct commerce, get supplies, and sailed south to enter the Baetica Province through the military port of Urci (today Almeria) or around to Gades (today Cadiz)

As illustrated in Figure 6, there were three Roman provinces in Hispania at the beginning of the first century: Tarraconensis (with Tarraco as its capital), Lusitania (with Emerita Agusta as its Capital), and Baetica (with Corduba as its capital). Of these, the most Romanized and safe province was Baetica, a "Senatorial Province," which is today's Community of Andalucía.

As a Senatorial Province, Baetica was represented by Senators in the Roman Senate and had a higher level of security, making it a safer province for its citizens, and as such, for Christian communities to be established and grow.

Few people today realize that Hispania, and in particular the Baetica Province, was vitally important to the Roman Empire during the time of Christ since it provided large amounts of agricultural, fish, and other food products to Rome's extensive empire. It also had an important shipping and transportation industry that was essential to trade and commerce throughout the empire.

Hispania came under Roman rule in 218 BC, but it was not until 19 BC, under the governance of Emperor Augustus, that the region rose in prominence. That's also when the Baetica Province became a full Roman Senatorial province.

Of special interest in our study is Tarraco (today's Tarragona, just south of Barcelona), which was then the Imperial Capital of the Province of Tarraconensis. It was protected by a military port that supported trade and commercial activities between Hispania and Rome. It was the main entry port for ships traveling to Hispania using Roman trade routes departing from the port of Ostia, the principal Roman port.

The Ostia-Tarraco trade route was important because it allowed ships to reach Hispania in four days, as compared to several weeks if travel was by land. It was also a very safe route since ships would travel through the Roman fortified ports in the islands of Corsica and Sardinia before reaching Tarraco[7].

Once in Tarraco, travelers would go south to the Baetica region using the regional trade route that took ships from Tarraco down to the Roman cities of Cartago Nova or Urci, both of which had military ports to protect Roman trade in the region.

Once in Tarraco, travelers would go south to the Baetica region using the regional trade route that took ships from Tarraco down to the Roman cities of Cartago Nova or Urci, both of which had military ports to protect Roman trade in the region. Cartago Nova had a larger level of trade and commercial activity than Urci, but Urci was closer to the Baetica province, and for Paul, this was potentially a more important factor given the large population of the province.

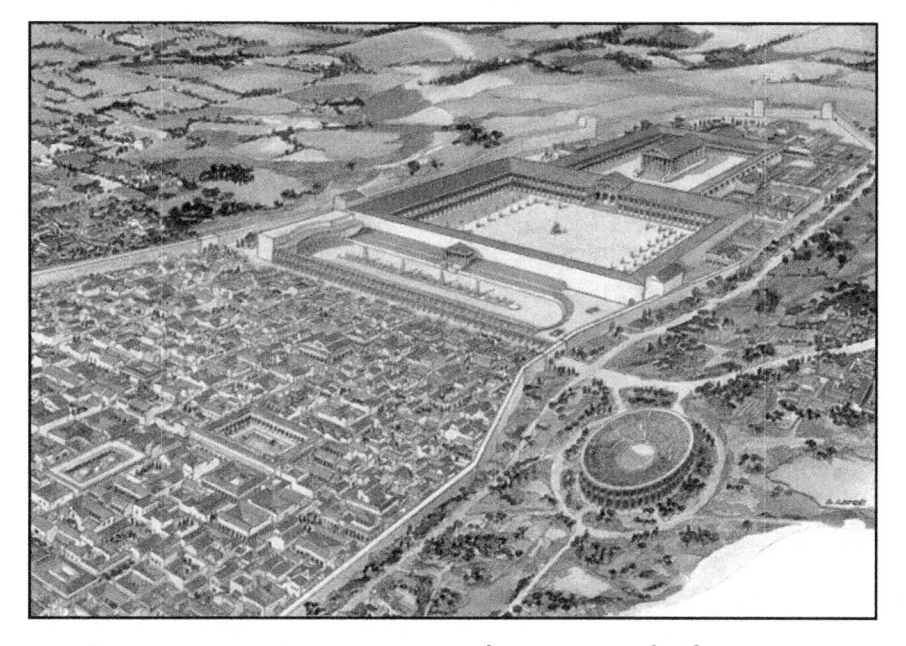

Fig. 7: Tarraco in Roman times, around 100 AD. Temple of Augustus in the top[8].

It's been well documented that Tarraco became one of Emperor Augustus favorite capitals since its people erected an impressive temple in his name (see Fig. 7). Because of its mild climate compared to Rome, he actually moved there for a period of his life in order to recuperate from an illness he had acquired.[9]

Today's cathedral of Tarragona was built on top of the ruins of that temple. Archeological excavations under the cathedral's main apse have confirmed the previous existence of the ancient temple. Visitors can actually see these ruins with special permission from the office of the Archbishop of Tarragona[10].

The City of Urci no longer exists but it was located in the same vicinity as today's City and Port of Almeria. Visitors to Almeria can actually see the walls of an ancient fortress, parts of which were built during the Islamic and Christian periods (Figure 8).

Fig. 8: Alcazaba de Almeria, here is where the old Roman fortress was set to protect the Roman Port City of Urci. (picture: Andalucía Office of Tourism)

Another potential route to reach the Baetica region was through the port of Cartago Nova (today's Cartagena, a thriving commercial port). There were land routes from either of these two cities that could be used to reach the city of Acci (today's Guadix), which had become an important crossroad for trade transported to and from the Baetica region and Rome.

In addition to Tarraco, the two other capital cities in Roman Hispania were Corduba (today's Cordoba) in the Baetica Province and Emerita Augusta (today's Merida) in the Lusitania Province. Corduba was of great importance since the Baetica Province had become very safe for Roman citizens, and as a result, had a thriving commercial and industrial presence. One of the critical elements to Corduba's success was the powerful river Baetis (today's Guadalquivir), which bordered the city and flowed through the other major cities of the province, including Hispalis (today's Seville), and continued down to the port city of Gades which was located on the Atlantic side of Hispania (today's Cadiz). From the port of Gades, ships could easily navigate back into the Mediterranean and reach Rome in approximately seven days.

Another important commercial center in the Baetica Province was the city of Astigi (today's Ecija), located only 55 kilometers southwest from Corduba, which developed into an important manufacturing and agricultural center. Astigi used the River Genil, one of the main tributaries of the River Baetis, to connect its products with those of Corduba and then transport them back to Rome through the Baetis. The 55 kilometers land-route between both cities was also well developed and that allowed for the evolution of Roman communities in both cities, which would later become important in the evolution of early Christian communities.

The above summary on how the Roman Empire was established and grew in the region of Hispania, and in particular the Baetica province, is significant because it explains the positive conditions that existed in this region for the growth of Christianity. Given the stability of the Baetica Province and of Hispania in general, the focus of the Roman governors of the region was on the growth of trade and commerce in commercial and manufacturing products. Most Roman governors in Hispania, therefore, had little interest in persecuting Christians, so when an edict came down from an Emperor, they mostly sought to make examples of a couple of Christian leaders but not destroy the entire community.

With such large populations of pagan gentiles, many of whom were tired of the many Roman gods they had to worship, combined with Jewish communities eager for the coming of a "Messiah," the conditions were fertile for a religion that preached salvation based on the belief that Jesus Christ was the Messiah, the Savior.

As an educated Roman citizen, there is no doubt Paul was aware of the very large gentile population of Hispania. This was particularly important for Paul's stated mission to bring the "Word" of Christ to the gentiles, and to the "... limits of the east and the west ..." of the then known world. It should be noted that in Roman times, Hispania was also known as the "limits of the west" of the world at the time[11]. This is an important point since in the original texts of the New Testament, as well as in other early Church documents, there are several references made to Paul's desire to spread the "Word" to the limits of the west.

With the economic stability and relative safety of the Baetica province, a large number of Christian communities were established in the region by the end of the third century. Ancient documents that have been preserved to today indicate that the density of Christians living in the Baetica province was among the highest, if not the highest, in early Christendom. Fig. 5 presented in the Introduction section of this book illustrated this point. For sure, given the documented results coming from certain Christian Councils that took place in this province, which we will cover later in the book, the advance precepts of what it meant to be a Christian were well developed in this province by the year 300 AD.

Based on the above discussion, then the obvious question that follows is to ask: When did the first Christian communities appeared in Hispania and who founded those communities? Did they grow out of a few converts from existing Jewish communities visited by Paul in his missionary trip, combined with gentile converts? Or, were they founded by another disciple of one of the 12 apostles? Or, did they evolve, as some believe, mostly from other missionaries settling in Hispania? Unfortunately, we don't have definitive answers to these questions, but we can connect a number of historical "dots" to reach an intelligent conclusion.

If we explore the possibilities, the only ancient tradition, other than Paul, that exists of an apostle traveling to Hispania began in the IX century. This tradition is based on the legend that the Apostle Saint James (Santiago in Spanish) had preached in the northern Galicia region of Hispania around the years 39-40AD but after he returned to Jerusalem was apprehended and executed. His disciples smuggled his bones out of Jerusalem and buried them in

Galicia in a large field named Compostela. The tradition was later expanded in the XIII century with the legend that the Virgin Mary had appeared to St. James in the Roman city of Caesarea Augusta (today's Zaragoza), in northern Hispania in the year 40 AD. (Note: the name Santiago derives from the Latin Sanct Iacobus, with iterations over centuries to Sanc Tiaco, and later combined to Santiago in Spanish; Saint James in English derives from the Italian Sanct Giacomo).

The tradition that Santiago visited the northern regions of Hispania is very strong and must be taken seriously. However, it should be noted that the Catholic Encyclopedia and a number of biblical historians have expressed skepticism given the historical difficulties for which this tradition is based[12]. It raises the question of why James would have been preaching in the relatively desolate northern regions of Hispania when it was well known at the time that the southern Senatorial Province of Baetica had a much, much larger population. In addition, the evidence of existing Jewish settlements all pointed to the southern regions of Hispania and not the northwest or northcentral regions. James' focus would have been to preach to Jewish communities since he, and the other 12 apostles, were not focused on converting the pagan gentiles at the time.

Only Paul had positioned himself as the "Apostle to the Gentiles," so it would make more sense that Paul, and not James, would have been in Hispania, especially in the southern Baetica region.

What historical records tell us is that in the year 40 AD, which is when the tradition says James preached in the northern regions of Hispania, there are no records of Jewish communities in that region. This was mostly a desolate region with a very low population. It is true that the city of Caesarea Augusta was a little further inland from the coastal imperial capital of Tarraco. Caesarea Augusta was a somewhat important city as a military outpost to guard the desolate northern regions of Hispania, but other than that, this was a mostly uninhabited region. As most biblical historians agree, it makes little sense that James would have been preaching there as opposed to having gone south to the Baetica province.

That said, there is no evidence or even oral tradition that St. James had been in the southern Baetica province, which is where Christianity grew very rapidly. In contrast, as covered in the next chapters, there is considerable written documentation from early Church "Fathers" outside of Hispania that it was Paul who made a missionary trip to Hispania. That documentation is augmented with the oral tradition from within Hispania that Paul indeed visited Tarraco and the southern Baetica province.

We don't want to diminish in any way the tradition that St. James had been in the northern regions of Hispania. We do, however, need to explore who would have been responsible for Christianity to have been planted so firmly and expand so rapidly throughout the Baetica province in the first 200 years AD. This would have taken someone very charismatic, someone with a high level of authority regarding this new religion, someone similar to a direct apostle of Jesus Christ himself.

There really is no strong tradition or documented references from early Church leaders that point to anyone other than Paul to have been that original source. That documentation will be provided in detail in the next chapters, but I simply make the point here that both St. James and St. Paul could have been in Hispania: James in the North and Paul in the South.

It is important therefore to continue exploring why Hispania was such fertile territory for the introduction of Christianity.

As the New Testament has recorded in a number of passages, the Apostles followed a pattern of first going to Jewish synagogues in the communities they were traveling through to preach the Word of Christ. They would address the Jewish congregation to explain the Word and how Jesus was the real Messiah. In Paul's case, since he was also focused on reaching gentiles, after an initial approach to Jewish communities he would intentionally also follow with preaching the Word to gentiles in those communities.

It is therefore important to examine the probability that Jewish communities existed in Hispania during Paul's times, or even before. The answer to this question is actually provided in the Old Testament, where we have specific passages that make references to Jewish settlements in Hispania. And those passages point to Jewish communities having been established in the southern region of Hispania several centuries before the birth of Jesus Christ.

Fig. 9: Painting showing King Solomon, 950 BC, who built the first Jewish Temple. He was responsible for also building a fleet of ships for naval expeditions in collaboration with the Phoenicians[13]

In 1-Kings 9:26-28, we see that around 950 BC, King Solomon formed an alliance with Hiram of Tyre, the king of the Phoenicians, to support each other's country with ships and sailors. In fact, Solomon had a fleet of trading ships that were manned in conjunction with Hiram's sailors, and once every three years they would return carrying gold, silver and ivory (2 Chronicles 9:21).

These Bible passages clearly indicate that Jewish sailors were traveling all over the Mediterranean and were reaching Hispania and other major trading outlets throughout the region. They were partnering with Phoenician sailors, who themselves had established settlements in the northern Africa region and in southern Hispania in order to protect and manage their commercial activities in the Mediterranean. This is a critical point since it would be logical to conclude that over a period of 950 years, Jewish communities would have settled in those regions.

It's important to note that Phoenician settlements have been uncovered by archeologists in the southern region of the Iberia Peninsula (Hispania), dated to around 800 BC.[14]

There is historical evidence, including maps developed by historians, supporting the premise mentioned above. As the map in Fig.10 shows, there were Phoenician and Greek ancient settlements throughout the Mediterranean, and they clearly show the southern region of Hispania to have been a major area of Phoenician settlements. It would only be logical then to conclude that Jewish sailors, and perhaps family members, would have also settle there.

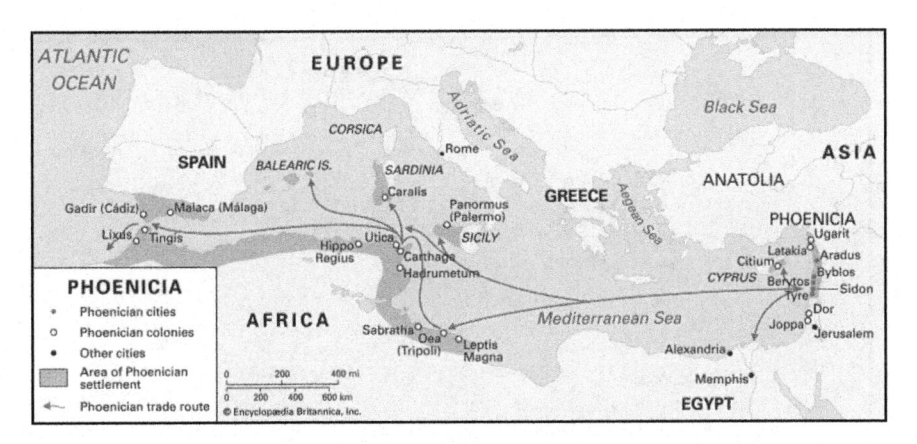

Fig. 10: From the time of King Solomon through 300 BC, Phoenician and Greek Colonies, were established to control trade routes. This map shows Phoenicians, with Jewish sailors as partners, established colonies in southern regions of Hispania, known as Tarshish during that period of time, 900 BC to 300 BC[15]

According to biblical historians, the southern region of Hispania was referred to as Tarshish in the time of King Solomon. This is the name mentioned in the Old Testament books of Jeremiah, Ezekiel, 1 Kings, and Jonah as a place where Jewish communities existed.

There is further evidence that Jewish communities had already been established by the years 64-66 AD in Hispania, which is when Paul would have been preaching there. This evidence is linked to the two separate Jewish expulsions by Roman emperors prior to 64 AD. The first of these expulsions was in the year 19 AD by Emperor Tiberius. This was followed by the expulsion by Emperor Claudius in the year 49 AD. Although it came after 64 AD, the most brutal of Jewish expulsions came in the year 70 AD under Emperor Nero's command to burn down Solomon's temple and destroy Jerusalem[16]. There's significant evidence that following each of these three expulsions many Jewish families immigrated to Hispania. This indicates that there must have been significant communities of Jews already in Hispania at that time.

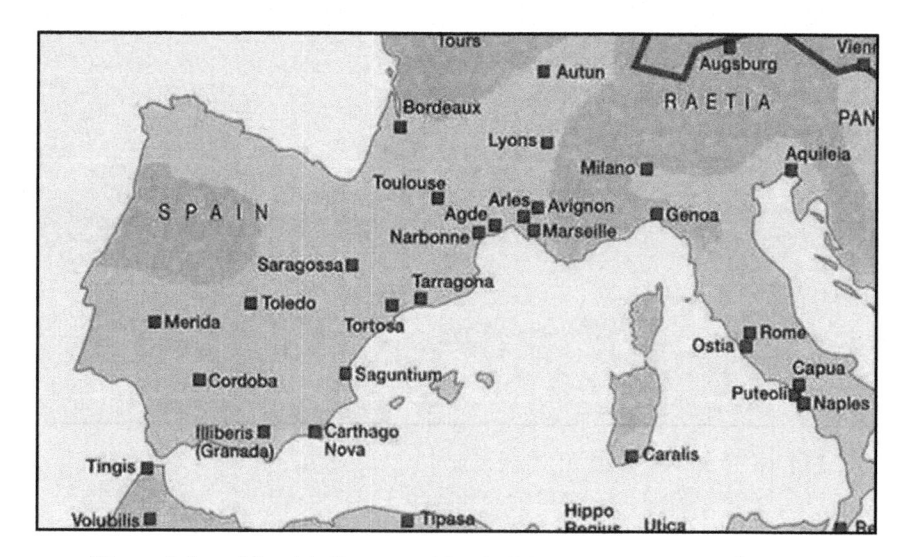

Fig. 11: Map of Jewish Communities in Hispania, 300 AD[17], shown as squares

As the map in Fig. 11 illustrates by the blue squares, there were multiple Jewish communities already established by the end of the 1st century in Hispania[18]. Notice that no Jewish communities existed in the northwest region, which is where Galicia and Asturias are located and where the tradition of St. James having preached there has been established. This map therefore reinforces the fact that the conditions existed for the seeds of Christianity to have been planted in the southern and eastern areas of Hispania.

With Jewish communities expecting the Messiah to appear any day, the news that he had arrived would have been of interest to these communities. The challenge for those preaching the Word of Jesus would have been to convince them that the Messiah was indeed Jesus, who offered a new vision of salvation.

If we're going to assert that Paul did make a missionary trip to Hispania, then establishing the fact that Jewish communities existed in Hispania during his time is important. In this regard, there's more specific and well-documented evidence that will be covered in later chapters that support this fact, providing support for Paul making his missionary trip in the first century.

Paul surely saw Hispania as fertile ground to convert Gentiles since he had to have known there were Jewish communities already established there. As an educated Roman citizen who was also Jewish, he must have been instructed at some point that there were Jewish communities as well as large population of gentiles in Hispania.

As will be explained in the following chapters, the large population of gentiles in Hispania was of critical importance to Paul. This point supports the premise that Paul had set a very high priority to travel to Hispania and that he was able to complete his desired missionary trip. Unfortunately, this was his last missionary trip. As soon as he returned to Rome, he was arrested as part of the brutal persecution of Christians launched by Nero and shortly after executed. The result was that he was never able to document his trip or write an Epistle to the Hispaniards.

Chapter 2

NEW TESTAMENT WRITINGS THAT SUPPORT PAUL'S HIGH PRIORITY MISSIONARY TRIP TO HISPANIA

Fig. 12: *St. Paul,* Painting by El Greco, 1606, El Greco Museum, Toledo Spain

A major challenge for Biblical historians over the years regarding the origins of Christianity in Hispania, as Spain was known in Roman times, is to answer two specific questions. The first is to identify who was responsible for first bringing the Word of Christ to the peninsula, and the second, to identify when the first established Christian communities originally appeared in Hispania. There are varying opinions on these two questions, but historians all agree that by the year 300 AD the southern Roman province of Baetica in Hispania had one of the most extensive accumulation of Christians communities in all of Christendom.

By this early point in Christian history, Hispania already had at least 37 well-established Christian communities, and at least 19 Bishops. We know this because of the detailed proceedings documented at the Council of Elvira that took place between the years 302-304 AD in the Roman town of Iliberis, today's Granada, Spain. A couple of these bishops became among the most important Christian leaders and theologians in early Christianity[19].

We need to keep in perspective that these communities evolved well before Roman Emperor Constantine legalized Christianity as a religion in the year 313. There were no speedways at that time, broadcast media did not exist, and you could not easily reproduce books or documents for wide distribution. In order for Christian communities to have flourished and spread so widely, we have to conclude that a couple of centuries before there was a very intense missionary effort responsible for its origins and rapid growth.

Many biblical historians believe that to have had such an impact by the end of the third century, this effort had to begin in the second half of the first century. It also had to have been led by a very charismatic missionary, or a group of assigned missionaries.

This point was strongly suggested by one of the most respected Church historians from the University of Granada in Spain, Fr. Manuel Sotomayor Muro, in his immensely important seven volume *History of the Church in Spain*[20], published in 1973. In this work, Fr.

Sotomayor explains the various scenarios on how Christianity could have reached Hispania. He provided the strong possibility that it could have been at the hand of an Apostle, or the direct disciple of one of the Apostles. He also mentioned it could have been by the many immigrants coming from Rome since Hispania was vital to Rome in commercial activities. In this regard, it would be logical to conclude Christian converts from other regions immigrated to Hispania during the first three centuries since it was a fairly safe place for Christians[21]. But this argument presupposes that Christians already knew that it was safe for them to travel there, so there had to have been Christian communities already established there very early on.

In contrast to the immigration argument, Fr. Sotomayor presented the strong possibility that it could have been the Apostle Paul responsible for introducing Christianity to Hispania[22]. In support of this premise, he dedicated an important section in the first volume of his work to include several important arguments that pointed to Paul having been in Hispania, but he stopped just short of making it a definitive statement.

There is a growing number of researchers,[23] including myself, that are now advancing the premise that Paul would have been indeed responsible for planting the seeds of Christianity in Hispania. Based on a number of historical accounts written in ancient church documents, there is a significant amount of direct and indirect documentation that point to Paul making a missionary trip to Hispania.

The challenge biblical historians have had for confirming in a definitive way that Paul made the missionary trip to Hispania, is that he never wrote an epistle to the "Hispaniards." In addition, no writings have survived from the early Christian churches within Hispania that mention his missionary trip. These two factors are used as arguments to support the premise he never visited Hispania, and in fact, most of the positive documentation that he made the trip comes from sources outside of Hispania.

These contrary arguments, however, have been analyzed in recent years in more detail and several very credible explanations have been developed as to why Paul never had a chance to write an epistle to the Hispaniards. These explanations, combined with the documentation from sources outside of Hispania, have resulted in a number of biblical historians concluding that it was highly probable that Paul did in fact make the trip between the years 64-66 AD[24,25,26]. Highlighting this conclusion was the result of the international conference, "Pablo, Fructuoso, and Early Christianity," held in 2008 in Tarragona. There were 30 theologians and biblical historians who came together to analyze the evidence that existed about Paul having been to Hispania, and in particular, entering through Tarraco, today's Tarragona.[27]

After conducting my own research, I have also concluded that there's a very high degree of certainty that Paul did make Hispania his last missionary trip. He likely spent one to two years there before returning to Rome after the brutal persecution of Christians had been launched by Emperor Nero. He was quickly arrested and shortly after executed by being beheaded[28], thereby never having the opportunity to write a letter to the communities he founded there.

In this chapter, a detailed analysis of the writings in the New Testament that point to the fact Paul had made Hispania his highest priority at this point in his mission will be provided. Other information will also be included to augment the biblical writings in order to provide a pathway that allows one to conclude, if properly analyzed, that Paul made his high-priority trip to Hispania. In subsequent chapters, evidence and writings from other sources will be provided to further support this conclusion. Here are the most important arguments extracted from New Testament writings:

- Hispania had one of the largest gentile populations in the Roman empire. Paul saw his specific mission as trying to convert gentiles since Jesus had very clearly instructed him to do so (Ephesians

3: 1-6; Acts 13: 46-48). Therefore, going to Hispania had to have been one of his highest priorities. It would make sense that after his three extensive missionary trips to the eastern provinces of the Roman empire, that he would turn to the western limits, with Hispania being by far the most important region.

- Paul, himself, highlights his high priority to spread the Word to the gentiles in Hispania in his letter to the Romans (Chapter 15). In this letter he expresses his strong intentions to make the trip to Hispania after first delivering the donations he had gathered from the faithful of Macedonia to the brothers in Jerusalem. On the way to Hispania, he planned on stopping to greet the faithful in Rome. However, he didn't have the chance to travel to Hispania on that occasion since he was arrested in Jerusalem after the Jewish leaders conspired to have him arrested when he entered the Temple there. After two years in jail in Caesarea, which was the Roman government center in Israel, he was sent to Rome where he spent two more years under Roman custody in "house-arrest" confinement.

- The positive ending to Paul's house-arrest in Rome, as expressed by Luke in Acts of the Apostles (Acts 28: 30-31), implies that he must have been set free at the end of those two years[29], setting the stage for him to travel to Hispania once he was liberated. This point has grown in acceptance by biblical historians, with the argument being: If Paul's expressed goal had been to travel to Hispania, why on earth would he not do so once he was set free in Rome after two years in house-arrest? Another argument presented by some historians is the possibility he was tried in Rome, but since he was a Roman citizen, instead of execution he was exiled to the farthest limits of the Empire. Hispania at the time was one of the so called "farthest limits of the empire," and a place Paul would then choose to go.

- In Paul's second letter to Timothy, his most trusted disciple, written shortly before he was executed (66-67AD), Paul stated that he "had completed the race," clearly implying he had accomplished everything he intended to do (2Timothy 4:6-7). This would imply he was able to complete his high priority trip to Hispania since Timothy would have certainly known how high a priority it was. Had he not made the trip to Hispania, Paul surely would have included that reference in his letter to Timothy, asking him to complete the mission for him. Instead, he makes the definitive statement of having "completed the race," which has been interpreted by many biblical historians that he must have certainly completed his high priority missionary trip to Hispania.

In this chapter, the four major arguments presented above, each extracted from the New Testament writings, will be explored individually since each is of great importance. Arguments made by distinguished biblical historians will be presented in their support. In addition, my own personal analysis from a researcher's point of view will also be presented. In later chapters additional information from other sources will be presented to establish the irrefutable conclusion Paul made the trip to Hispania.

It is critically important, however, that we begin this chapter by first providing a quick profile of Paul in order to make readers of this book aware of his tenacity and persistent character. Once we understand who Paul was, and the mandate given to him by Jesus to reach out and convert the gentiles (pagans), the arguments of why he made the missionary trip to Hispania will become clearer.

A. What does the New Testament say about Paul? Why is he referred to as an Apostle?

St. Paul is undoubtedly one of the most important historical individuals in Western Christian culture. Thousands of books have been written about him, many portraying him as the real source for championing Christianity as a separate religion, established by Jesus Christ, and not as a sect of Judaism.

As explained in Acts of the Apostles and in Paul's own letters, he was known by the Jewish name of Saul, a dedicated member of the Jewish sect known as Pharisees. As a teenager, he was sent to the well-known Jewish school headed by Gamaliel, a Pharisee Doctor of Jewish Law (Acts 22:3). Then as a young man in his mid-20's, Saul became one of the most ardent and passionate persecutors of Christians. However, during a trip to the City of Damascus to find and incarcerate Christians, he had a jolting encounter with Jesus. This encounter left him totally blind for several days until his sight was restored by a Damascus disciple of Jesus named Ananias (Acts 9: 13-19). Following this encounter, Paul had a number of additional encounters with Jesus where he received his messages through what he termed as "divine revelation."

Paul was therefore never one of the Twelve Apostles. As a result of his encounters with Jesus and divine revelation, he developed his own understanding of Jesus' message of salvation, based on love and faith in Jesus as our Savior. He "self-proclaimed" himself an Apostle of Jesus, with authority given to him directly from Jesus and God the Father (Galatians 1:1-5). He also proclaimed himself to be the Apostle to the pagan-gentiles, a point Peter and the Apostles eventually accepted (Galatians 2:7). This was different from the position of the Twelve Apostles who at the beginning focused Christ's teachings to the Jewish community as a version of Judaism, a version that in their view added to the Law of Moses (Acts 9:1-31).

Another very important point about Paul's missionary focus is that he depended on the Holy Spirit to guide him. Both in Acts of the Apostles as well as in Paul's letters, the references to the Holy Spirit's influence comes across over and over. After spending time in a community and establishing a following, Paul would depend on the Holy Spirit to take over and continue the work of growing that newly established Christian community.

We know that Paul was an amazing and tireless missionary who, as documented by his letters and Acts of the Apostles, travelled over

10,000 miles during his missionary trips. He had an extensive record of convincing new converts into the religion and of embedding into those converts a passionate belief in Christ.

Paul worked relentlessly to spread the Word of Jesus and was clearly the most effective and determined missionary of Apostolic times. As was his custom in the communities where he was successful in converting new "believers," he would establish leaders in charge of those communities and counted on the Holy Spirit to help them grow those communities.

A fact very few Christians even today realize is that Paul's missionary legacy between the years 37 AD to 66/67 AD began before the Gospels were even written. Most biblical historians agree that the gospels were written sometime between the years 65-100 AD.[30] Paul's letters are therefore the earliest recorded documents about Jesus and his teachings, influenced of course by Paul's understanding of Jesus' messages for salvation.

Paul therefore did not have the benefit of the Gospels to further study and grasp the meaning of those messages. His understanding of Jesus as the Messiah, and the ramifications of his suffering and crucifixion in reference to our salvation, was developed through his divine encounters/revelations with Jesus.

It is true that around 39-40 AD, Paul spent 15 days in Jerusalem early in his ministry speaking with Peter and James. This James was identified by Paul as the brother of Jesus whom Paul called a pillar of the Church of Jerusalem, but this was not James the Greater, one of the original Apostles. Paul met with them to learn more of the personal interactions they had with Jesus. Based on Paul's letters, however, it appears he did not learn a great deal more than what he had learned from his own divine revelations (Galatians 2:6).

Fig. 13: Paul writing his Epistles. He normally wrote them after his trips (*Saint Paul,* by Valentin de Boulogne, cir, 1618; Museum of Fine Arts, Houston)

To this point, it is very important to note that Paul was the first to realize that Jesus' sacrifice on the Cross to redeem our sins meant that *faith in Jesus as our Savior and Redeemer* was the only thing required to enter heaven and be saved. Later in his ministry, he even preached that the "Law of Moses" was no longer required to be saved. The Catholic Church, of course, has taken Paul's position and enhanced it with the other writings from the Old and New Testaments, especially those writings from the Evangelists and letters from the other Apostles. The Church's deep understanding includes the fact that a person' conduct and actions must also be taken into consideration in addition to the belief in Jesus as our Savior and Redeemer.

Paul's position, however, caused tremendous friction with the Twelve Apostles, including Peter and James who still believed that following the Law of Moses was critical to salvation. Again, we need to remember that Paul was not one of the Twelve, and since he was known as one of the main persecutors of Christians, the Apostles were skeptical of his authority to preach the Word of Christ. It is true that the Apostles would become aware of his conversion in Damascus after Ananias surely informed other Christians in the community; however, we can understand why the Apostles would have been very distrustful of Paul and his message, and why they began to aggressively question his authority.

Paul shows his determination and tenacious character when he responds to the Apostles lack of trust in his message. The Apostles had been growing increasingly indignant with his message that adhering to the "Law" was no longer necessary. Under the authority of Peter and James, delegations of disciples were sent to the areas where Paul had been preaching to inform those communities that following the Law was vital if one wanted to be saved. (Paul's Epistle to the Galatians)

Those disciples first went into the region of Galatia, and given Paul's close relationship with the Galatians, he quickly found out they were trying to undermine his version of the Word. Those disciples even contradicted Paul's authority to represent the Word of Jesus. Paul then responded by sending a stern letter to the Galatians, first establishing his authority, followed by admonishing "his converts" for listening to the message from these disciples. He starts his letter with a direct rebuke of those disciples:

> "Paul, an Apostle—sent neither by human commission nor from human authorities, but through Jesus Christ and God the Father, who raised him from the dead—and all the members of God's family who are with me, to the churches of Galatia: Grace to you and peace from God our Father and the Lord Jesus Christ, who gave himself for our sins to set us free from the present evil age, according to the will of our God and Father to whom be the glory, forever and ever. Amen." (Galatians 1:1-5)

Paul's opening in this letter was meant for both the Church of Galatia as well as sending a strong message to the Apostles and their disciples. His authority was based on Divine Revelation from Jesus himself and not from any human being; i.e., from any of the Apostles. As explained in Acts of the Apostles, Peter and James eventually accepted part of Paul's argument, especially that new converts into the religion would not need to be circumcised as required by the Law.

This decision was reached during the Council of Jerusalem in 49/50 AD, chaired by James. At the completion of the Council, James sent a letter to the "believers" in Antioch in Syria explaining the decision that gentile (pagan) believers would not need to be circumcised (Acts 15: 12-21). The message in this letter was relayed to other communities, especially where Paul had preached.

It's important to establish early in this chapter that Paul's persistent and tenacious character was a crucial trait that pushed him to an unwavering commitment to his mission: **To tirelessly spread the Word of Jesus to the limits of the east and the west.** This character trait will serve as a vital argument for supporting the premise that Paul eventually conducted a missionary trip to Hispania. In other words, given this was a very high priority for him, his persistent character would have driven him to not let anything stand in the way and to eventually make the trip.

As will be explained in section-B below, Paul had a very clear mandate to spread the Word to pagans, also referred to as gentiles. In that regard, the Baetica province being the only Senatorial province of the three Hispania provinces, had one of the largest population of gentiles in the Roman empire. For sure, Paul must have known that fact, and this would have led him to set a very high priority to go there.

B. Bible Passages on Paul's Mission to Convert Gentiles based on Direction from Jesus

It is important to recap that in Chapter-1 the significance of Hispania to the Roman Empire was highlighted. In particular, documentation was presented of the importance of the Baetica Province itself, since it was a highly "Romanized" Senatorial Province. This is a vital point since

Hispania had a very high population of gentiles, and Paul, as a Roman citizen, could have easily traveled to and throughout the region.

An explanation was also provided that Hispania had the foundations for the establishment of Christian communities since Jewish Communities already existed there from before apostolic times. It was the practice of Paul, and of the other apostles, to first go to the Jewish synagogues to proclaim the Word of Jesus to the Jews. Paul expanded this practice and also preached to the gentiles after first speaking in synagogues.

Keep in mind that during the very early stages of Christianity, this new religion had strong connections to Judaism since Jesus was Jewish, and the Jewish religion was waiting for a Messiah to arrive. It would have therefore been a logical step for Paul and the apostles to first attempt to speak to Jews in their synagogues. Paul quickly learned, however, that the Jewish leadership would not listen to him, so he turned his attention to gentiles since Christ had specifically instructed him that the gentiles would also be heirs to God's grace. This point is made clear in Paul's letter to the Ephesians:

> "[2]Surely you have heard about the administration of God's grace that was given to me for you, [3] that is, the mystery made known to me by revelation, as I have already written briefly. ... [6] This mystery is that through the gospel, the Gentiles are heirs together with Israel, members together of one body, and together sharers in the promise of Christ Jesus." (Ephesians 3: 2-3, 6)

In fact, Paul's mission to focus on the gentiles is clarified in Acts 13, 46-48, where together with Barnabas, he addresses Jewish leaders, explaining they first needed to speak the Word to them, but would now turn their mission to converting the gentiles:

> [46] "Then Paul and Barnabas answered them boldly: 'We had to speak the Word of God to you first. Since you reject it and do not

consider yourselves worthy of eternal life, we now turn to the Gentiles. [47] For this is what the Lord has commanded us:

'I will also make you a light for the Gentiles so that my salvation may reach to the ends of the earth.' (see Isaiah: 49, 6)

[48] When the Gentiles heard this, they were glad, and honored the word of the Lord; and all who were appointed for eternal life believed." (Acts: 13, 46-48)

We can therefore understand why Hispania would have been of such high priority for Paul. This was one of the highest populated regions in the Roman empire, estimated at 5 million in apostolic times[31], effectively all pagan gentiles. For this reason, Hispania had to have been a very high priority for Paul, which is an essential premise being presented in this book.

Fig. 14: Paul speaking to Jewish leaders[32]

Paul was an educated Roman citizen, and as he said himself: *"... a Hebrew from the tribe of Benjamin and a well-trained Pharisee"* (Philippians 3:5).

Paul was surely well informed of the significance of Hispania to the Roman Empire and its status as a Senatorial Province. Reaching the gentiles there would have finally fulfilled his mission of spreading the Word to the extremities of the east and the west.

C. Letter to Romans Explains Why Reaching Hispania was a High Priority for Paul

Hispania was therefore virgin territory for preaching to the gentiles given its very dense population, but for Paul, the fact that no other Apostle had preached there made it an even higher priority. In his letter to the Romans, written while Paul was still in Corinth around the year 58 AD[33], Paul clearly expresses the importance of these two very high priorities:

a) his focus on spreading the gospel of God to Gentiles, and
b) his priority was to conduct a missionary trip to Hispania, but he would first stop in Rome to meet the Christian community there, and hopefully they would help him with his plans to get to Hispania

Paul's letter to the Romans is often misunderstood. Many biblical historians, priests, and pastors focus much more on Paul's writing on his views of salvation based on Jesus Christs divine revelations to him. If we analyze his entire letter, however, one of his main point was really to get to Hispania. The problem is that Paul doesn't say that until Chapter-15.

Paul must have known that the most logical place to launch his missionary trip to Hispania was to launch it from Rome. Since he knew he would stop in Rome, he uses the letter to introduce himself, and also takes the opportunity to expand on his views on salvation since the Romans had never heard from him directly. Beginning with the first chapter, he makes sure to explain that he's an apostle through the grace of God and explain his goal of spreading the Word of Jesus Christ to gentile communities:

"¹Paul, a servant of Christ Jesus, called to be an apostle and set apart for the gospel of God, ² the gospel he promised beforehand through his prophets in the Holy Scriptures ³ regarding his Son, who as to his earthly life, was a descendant of David, ⁴ and who through the Spirit of holiness was appointed the Son of God in power by his resurrection from the dead: Jesus Christ our Lord. ⁵ Through him we received grace and apostleship to *call all the Gentiles* to the obedience that comes from faith for his name's sake. ⁶ And you also are among those Gentiles who are called to belong to Jesus Christ. ⁷ To all in Rome who are loved by God and called to be his holy people: Grace and peace to you from God our Father and from the Lord Jesus Christ. (Rom 1: 1-7).

Paul then proceeds to expand between Chapter-1 through Chapter-14 his views on what Jesus had instructed him through divine revelation, which included becoming the apostle to the gentiles. It's not until he reaches Chapter-15 that Paul then states that for a long time he had wanted to visit Rome and would do so on his way to Hispania. So, going to Hispania was actually his main goal, and visiting the Roman community in "passing" would allow him to finally get to know that community. He was in effect using his high-priority trip to Hispania as an opportunity to meet the Roman Christians, and further, hoping they would help him plan his trip to Hispania.

This very important point has been missed by many biblical historians. For Paul, visiting Hispania was the higher priority since his letter to the Romans, which turned out to be very important for expressing his views on salvation, was a personal introduction to the Roman Christian community. His letter would inform them about his perspective of this new religion based on divine revelation given to him by Jesus.

We provide here the full passages of Chapter-15 that explain these points, dividing the two major priorities, preaching to gentiles and reaching Hispania, so readers can appreciate his clear determination to accomplish both:

Romans: 15, 14-21—Bringing the Gospel to Gentiles

[14] "And concerning you, my brethren, I myself am also convinced that you yourselves are full of goodness, filled with all knowledge, and able also to admonish one another. [15]But I have written very boldly to you on some points, so as to remind you again, *because of the grace that was given me from God,* [16]*to be a minister of Christ Jesus to the gentiles,* ministering as a priest the gospel of God that my offering of the gentiles might become acceptable and sanctified by the Holy Spirit.

[17]Therefore in Christ Jesus I have found reason for boasting in things pertaining to God. [18]For I will not presume to speak of anything except what Christ has accomplished through me, resulting in the *obedience of the gentiles by word and deed,* [19]in the power of signs and wonders, in the power of the Spirit; so that from Jerusalem and round about as far as Illyricum, I have fully preached the gospel of Christ. [20]*And thus I aspired to preach the gospel, not where Christ was already named, that I might not build upon another man's foundation* [21], but as it is written,

'They who *had no news of him shall see,* and they *who have not heard shall understand.'"* (see Isaiah: 52, 15)

Continuing, keep in mind Paul writes his letter while in Corinth and clearly expresses plans to go to Hispania, Romans 15:22-29:

[22] "For this reason I have often been hindered from coming to you; [23] but now, with no further place for me in these regions, and since I have had for many years a longing to come to you,

> ²⁴*when I go to Hispania—for I hope to see you in passing, and to be helped on my way there by you,* when I have first enjoyed your company for a while— ²⁵but now, I am going to Jerusalem serving the saints. ²⁶For Macedonia and Achaia have been pleased to make a contribution for the poor among the saints in Jerusalem. ²⁷Yes, they were pleased to do so, and they are indebted to them. For if the gentiles have shared in their spiritual things, they are indebted to minister to them also in material things. ²⁸Therefore, when I have finished this, and have put my seal on this fruit of theirs, *I will go on by way of you to Hispania.* ²⁹And I know that when I come to you, I will come in the fullness of the blessing of Christ."

These passages leave no doubt that Paul had a very strong intention, and had placed a very high priority, to get to Hispania on his mission of spreading the Word to gentiles.

He needed, however, to first go to Jerusalem to deliver the funds that had been collected for the "... *poor among the saints in Jerusalem.*" What he did not expect was that upon arriving in Jerusalem, the Jewish leadership had planned to create disturbances and attribute them to him.

They got their first chance soon after he entered Jerusalem, accusing him of creating a major disturbance in the Temple and of acts against the sovereignty of Rome (Acts 21: 30-40). He was first arrested by the Temple guards and later turned over to the Roman governor to be tried under Roman law.

That would have been around the end of 58 AD or beginning of 59 AD.

Now that he was under arrest, his plans to reach Hispania would have been delayed, but not necessarily deterred. There is no doubt that Paul's own letter to the Romans clearly highlight that Hispania was of his highest priority to reach.

But, how would Paul have known this region had such a high concentration of gentiles? There is significant documentation from this period that provide evidence Hispania was a well-known major population center, especially its southern region.

We can begin by explaining that the Baetica Province, in the southern region of Hispania, had one of the highest densities in the Roman empire. Fig. 15 below, shows a map developed by a Roman Empire historian of Roman settlements around the years 100-150AD. It should be noted that during most of this period, the Roman Empire was ruled by two emperors who were born in Italica, in the Baetica Province of Hispania: Emperor Trajan, who governed from the years 98 – 117, and Emperor Hadrian, who governed from 117 – 138. Both are considered among the best rulers of the Roman Empire.

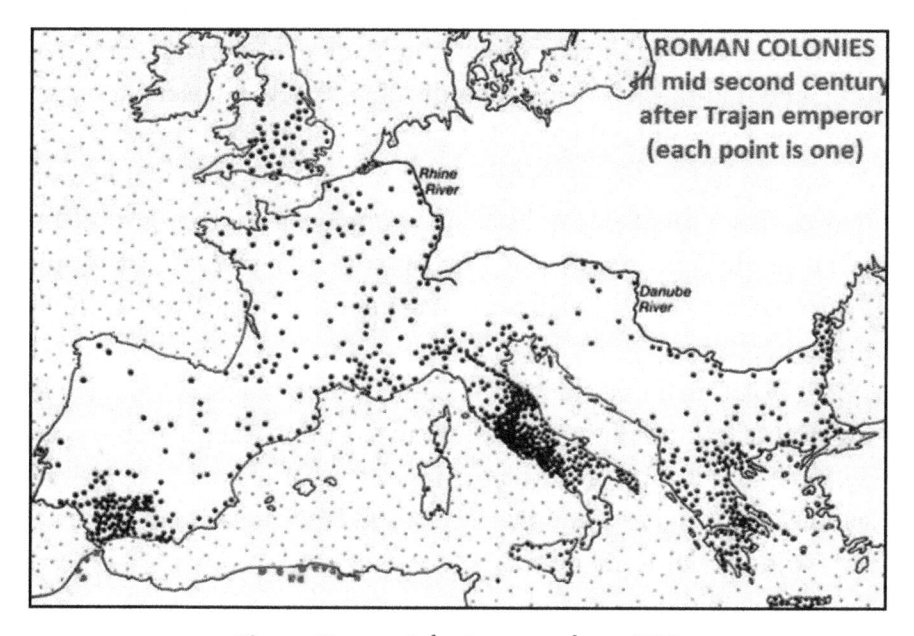

Fig. 15: Roman Colonies around 100 AD[34]

This map clearly shows the high density of colonies and settlements in the southern Baetica province of Hispania. This map provides a very strong argument that if anyone was to go to Hispania to try to convert its population, it would only make sense to go to the province of Baetica. It was the safest and most densely populated province in the region, and one of the most densely populated in the Empire. The map therefore supports the strategy used by Paul of going to the Baetica Province.

Given the above geographical and historical analysis, many biblical historians agree that although you cannot ignore the strong oral tradition that exists of St. James having been in northern Hispania, the most logical conclusion is that the Apostle Paul was a more likely candidate to have made a missionary trip to Hispania. The direct and indirect documentation that exist from the early Church, both written as well as oral, point very strongly to Paul having made the trip to Hispania. He had established a strategy of concentrating efforts in the areas of highest population of gentiles, and Hispania was obviously high on his radar. He would have entered through Tarraco, the Imperial Capital of the Tarraconensis Province (today's Tarragona), and likely spent some time there since it had a small Jewish community but also a large population of gentiles. Afterwards, he sailed down to the heavily populated Baetica Province, which as has been shown, also included some Jewish communities.

I have never seen a map similar to Fig. 15, used by a biblical historian. It actually raises significantly the credibility of why Hispania and the Baetica Province was of such high priority for Paul to travel there. As we can see, there is no doubt that it had one of the largest population densities in the Roman Empire. That's the reason why in Fig. 5, shown in the "Introduction" section of this book, we can connect with Fig. 15 and see that there must have been an organic evolution of Christianity. Fig. 5 provided a historically documented map illustrating that the Baetica Province had potentially one of the highest concentration of Christians by the year 300 AD, and Fig. 15 provides the evidence of how it must have started.

D. Acts of the Apostles by Luke: Paul is Jailed and Spends the Next Four to Five Years Under Roman Detention

In an extensive and detailed narrative by Luke in Acts (Chs. 23 and 24), following Paul's arrest in the Temple, he is brought in front of Roman governor Marcus Antonius Felix who decides to imprison and keep him in house arrest in Caesarea, the Roman administrative center for Israel. That was around the years 59-60 AD. Felix keeps him there for two years with little access to the outside world, while also trying to extort money from him in return for his liberty[35].

With the passage of those two years, Felix was replaced with a new governor, Porcius Festus. Fearing that his imprisonment would continue under Festus, Paul decided to claim his rights to be tried as a Roman citizen by Caesar's tribunal (Acts 25, 11). Festus agreed to his request, interpreting Paul's request that he should be tried in Rome. That was approximately the year 60-61 AD.

After the logistics were finally arranged for Paul's trial and trip to Rome, the long and arduous journey to the imperial capital began. The journey was described in breathtaking details by Luke (Acts 27: 1-31 through Acts 28: 1-16). Not only did Luke include extensive interactions between Paul and the soldiers keeping custody over him, but he covers in detail the sinking of the ship they were on, and the subsequent washing ashore of all the passengers in the island of Malta. Eventually, after a number of additional obstacles and encounters, Paul finally makes it to Rome, approximately by the year 62AD[36].

From this point in Acts, and after so much detail provided by Luke throughout the entire book of Acts, especially in describing Paul's journey to Rome, Luke's version of what came next is strangely lacking in detail. Now that he's nearing the end of the entire book, he suddenly switches to providing very scant account of what should have been very important passages. The first important passage is the encounter Paul had with leaders from the Jewish community in Rome, whom, as Luke briefly explains, informed Paul they had not received any negative information on him from Judea:

"We have not received any letters from Judea concerning you, and none of our people who have come from there has reported or said anything bad about you," (Acts 28: 21).

This is a very telling passage since the reason Paul was in jail was because of the accusation by Jewish leaders in Jerusalem that Paul had been preaching a new religion that plotted against Rome. If no one from Jerusalem was coming to enforce these charges, then Roman law would have required that Paul be set free.

A few passages later, without any further explanation, Luke inexplicably and abruptly ends Chapter 28 with a short, positive, and simple assertion that Paul remained in Rome under house-arrest for two more years.

This simple statement, listed here, not only ends the chapter but also ends the entire book of Acts of the Apostles:

> [30] "For two whole years Paul stayed there in his own rented house and welcomed all who came to see him. [31] He proclaimed the kingdom of God and taught about the Lord Jesus Christ—with all boldness and without hindrance!" (Acts 28: 30-31).

Fig. 16: Paul Speaks to visitors in Rome while in house-arrest[37]

Biblical historians over the centuries have tried to rationalize why Luke would end this chapter, and the entire Book of Acts, without making further references to what happened to Paul after those two years in house-arrest. The fact he used the past-tense in the closing sentence of Acts for the words "stayed" and "welcomed" indicates he was out of house arrest after two years. Wouldn't Luke have known if Paul finally went through a trial? Was he sentenced or was he placed in full liberty? If he was placed in liberty, where did he go? If none of the Jewish leaders from Jerusalem were coming to charge him, wouldn't the charges be dropped?

The positive tone of this ending would lead any researcher to conclude Paul must have been set free at the end, otherwise, with all the other extensive details he provides in Acts, Luke would have certainly included the details and results of a trial.

The obvious question a researcher would then ask is: if Paul was set free, and since he had placed a very high priority to preaching to the gentiles in Hispania, why in the world would he go anywhere else now that he was in Rome and so close geographically to Hispania? By his own accounts in his letter to the Romans, he was "done" preaching in the east, and now was focused on going to the extreme west, which in Roman times was Hispania.

Given the positive ending to Acts, the logical conclusion we can deduce is that Paul was placed in liberty right after the end of his house arrest. This would have been around the year 64-65 AD. Many biblical historians are also coming to the same conclusion.

It is not known what year Luke wrote Acts, but historians all agree that it would have been after the end of Paul's first Roman imprisonment; i.e., sometime after 64-65 AD. Some have suggested that he wrote it while he was with Paul two years later during Paul's second and last imprisonment in Rome, around 66-67 AD. Other's have suggested that he wrote it after Paul's death, 69-70 AD, or even later. It is therefore unimaginable that Luke would not have concluded the last chapter in Acts with the trial and its results, if in fact, the trial had been the conclusion after two years of house arrest.

E. Paul must have been set free

Therefore, with such a positive ending, many historians have concluded that Paul must have been placed in liberty[38].

I have also reached that same conclusion. It is important to note here that under Roman law, an individual could not be imprisoned for more than two years without having those that charged him/her appear in court to present their case[39]. If we consider what was happening in the Roman Empire around the years 61-64 AD, there was tremendous turmoil in Jerusalem, driven by constant Jewish revolts of various Jewish factions.

It is not only probable, but very likely, that as a result of the turmoil caused by these Jewish revolts, the Jewish leadership that levied charges against Paul in Jerusalem would not have taken the chance to show up in Rome. That would have also placed them in danger of being charged for the Jewish revolts in Jerusalem.

In the process of charging Paul, the Jewish leaders themselves could have been thrown in jail. With no one to come forward to charge Paul, which is clearly implied in Acts 28: 21 and Acts 28, 30-31, Roman authorities would have therefore been obligated to let Paul go free.

Some biblical historians, however, have recently pointed to a second potential scenario as a possible explanation for why Paul was not tried or executed at the end of the two years. These historians have hypothesized that Roman authorities would not have necessarily placed Paul in full liberty since he was known to be a controversial and contentious figure wherever he went. There were lesser sentences than capital punishment that could have been levied, and these called for the accused to be exiled to the outer limits of the Roman Empire.[40] Those sentences could be levied for a limited amount of time, or for the life of the accused. Since Hispania was in the outer limits of the empire, and in fact considered to be geographically the end of the known world, it was one of the places these exiles were sent to. It could certainly have been a place where

Paul would have been exiled to. Since Paul wanted to go there, he might have even requested to be sent to Hispania if that sentence was indeed implemented.

In either case, there is a two-year period, from 64-66 AD, following the end of his two-year house-arrest in Rome, where there is no information of Paul's whereabouts. There are no writings from him that would give a specific clue to where he went. Some historians have theorized that Paul was never set free and he was simply kept in jail for those two additional years. But this would go counter to the strict laws of Rome that he needed to be adjudicated after two years without anyone bringing charges. He was definitely either set free, or he was exiled, and in either case likely headed for Hispania.

It is not until Paul writes his second letter to Timothy and the letter to Titus, that we again have news of Paul. Based on their content, biblical historians have dated these letters to around the year 66 or 67 AD, two years after he was set free. At the time he wrote those letters, he was now clearly back in a Roman jail, and the tone of his message indicated that he expected his life to end soon (see next section, 2 Timothy 4: 6–8).

It is clear, therefore, that there are two missing years, 64-66 AD, where he was neither in prison nor that we have any information of his whereabouts.

Many biblical historians have recently pointed to the fact Paul certainly had enough time to go to Hispania during those two years.[41] Since it has already been established that this was a very high priority for him, we can "connect-the-dots" as researchers and conclude that this was a very high probability that he actually completed the trip.

It would make very little sense that he would do anything else. If he was now so close to Hispania, and with two years in house-arrest to plan his highly prioritized trip with guests coming in and out, he would not only have planned the trip but also recruited some followers to go with him. What was he to do? Go back to Jerusalem where both the Jews and the Romans could arrest him again? Go back to other churches he had founded and leave behind the chance to travel to Hispania to establish churches where the Word of Christ had not yet reached? The only thing that makes sense is that he would have gone to Hispania.

As researchers, we can also address the argument made by some that a letter from Paul to the "Hispaniards" has never surfaced. This argument is used to conclude that he never made the trip. If we take into consideration what was going on at the time, together with the customs, traditions and practices, this argument can be easily discredited.

The first explanation is that Paul would have normally written his letter to the Hispaniards after his trip. Based on the conclusion of many biblical historians, this was his last missionary trip, and as soon as he returned to Rome, he was apprehended and executed following Nero's orders to persecute Christians. Keep in mind that Roman authorities knew him to be a controversial Christian leader, so he would have been quickly apprehended. Paul's own comments in his last letter, written to his disciple Timothy (see next section), painted a grim picture that the end was near.

Consideration must also be given to the fact that the most common method of communication in early Christian times was through word of mouth. The concept that there should have been a proliferation of writings from Paul or others is simply not an overwhelming element of the reality of those times.

Combine these points with the additional fact many early writings have never survived. There were over 300 years of Roman rule during early Christianity in which multiple persecutions by Roman emperors were launched. Many books and relics from that period would have been destroyed by the Romans. The same occurred during the 500 years of Islamic rule in most of Hispania, from 756 to 1248. It has been well documented that early in their occupation of Hispania, Islamic rulers launched vicious initiatives to destroy Christian writings and relics.

So then, what other written biblical evidence would then lead us to believe he made it to Hispania?

In the next section of this chapter, section-F, an analysis is made of the specific message Paul sent when he writes his second letter to Timothy. In that letter, Paul alludes to having completed everything he wanted to do, which many biblical historians agree is a strong indication he completed his high-priority missionary trip to Hispania.

F. Paul's Message to Timothy: 2Tim 4:6-8, Paul Implies He Has Accomplished Everything He Intended to do

It is generally accepted by biblical historians that Paul wrote his second letter to Timothy during his second and final incarceration in Rome, in 66/67 AD. The tone of this letter clearly indicates that Paul was expecting to be executed and that the end was near. Timothy had been one of his most trusted disciples and one to whom Paul could open his heart to provide final instructions.

Fig. 17: Painting—Paul in Prison with Luke after Returning to Rome, Writing Letter to Timothy[42]

Paul's message in 2Tim 4:6-8, provide very significant and direct testimony from Paul. He not only expressed the end was at hand, but that he had accomplished everything he had set out to do:

> [6] "For I am already being poured out like a drink offering, and the time for my departure is near. [7] I have fought the good fight, *I have finished the race*, I have kept the faith. [8] Now there is in store for me the crown of righteousness, which the Lord, the righteous Judge, will award to me on that day ..." (2Tim 4:6-8).

At such a critical moment, when Paul was pouring out all his emotions, the only conclusion I can reach of Paul's assertion to Timothy that he had "finished the race" is that he was able to accomplish everything he had planned to do. This conclusion has also been interpreted the same way by many biblical historians. Keep in mind that Timothy had been with Paul through the most difficult times, Paul even referred to him as his "dearly beloved son," clearly documenting how close they were (2Tim 1:2-3).

The very critical point here is that Timothy had to have known of Paul's high priority to travel to Hispania. For Paul to mention, "I have finished the race ...," without any inference of disappointment for not evangelizing in Hispania gives a very compelling testimony to support that Paul visited Hispania. If Paul had not been able to go to Hispania, wouldn't he have asked Timothy to do it for him and "finish" his race?

This brings us to a very important point. One of the most difficult challenges Christian historians have is to accurately place all the early writings and documents in their proper historical context. This includes placing them not only in the proper time frame, but also in the context of other writings and other historical documents that exist. What makes it even more challenging for historians, is that there were many persecutions of Christians in which written documents and relics were destroyed. Historians can therefore only use those writings that survived to position them in context with each other, and many of those that survived were considered by the Church to be either heretical or not inspired by God.

We must then take 2Tim 4, 6-8 in the context of Paul's clear intentions to evangelize in Hispania. As has been shown, there is no doubt that this was a high priority for Paul, and one that Timothy must have been well aware of. So, when Paul tells Timothy that he had "... finished the race," the obvious historical context we can place on this statement is that he had crossed the finish line and accomplished everything he intended to do. This had to include going to Hispania.

Combining this conclusion with the other biblical references presented in this chapter and adding the evidence that will be presented in the following chapters, allows for a clear deduction, from a researcher's point of view, that Paul likely completed the trip to Hispania.

In the next chapters I will include the evidence provided by the documented writings of Pope Clement I, the Muratorian Fragment, the Apocryphal Gospel of Peter, and the other documented writings from six Doctors of the Church, clearly implying he was able to "finish the race."

CHAPTER 3

EVIDENCE PAUL MADE THE TRIP PROVIDED BY THREE EARLY INDEPENDENT DOCUMENTS FROM THE FIRST AND SECOND CENTURY

A. **LETTER FROM CLEMENT, BISHOP OF ROME, YEAR 96 AD**
B. **THE MURATORIAN FRAGMENT, FIRST HALF OF SECOND CENTURY**
C. **THE APOCRYPHAL GOSPEL OF PETER, FIRST HALF OF SECOND CENTURY**

As has already been mentioned, there are a growing number of biblical historians that point to the high probability that between the years 64 and 66 AD, Paul actually carried out his missionary trip to Hispania.[43,44] They base these assertions on a number of arguments, some of which include the biblical writings mentioned in the previous chapter, and others on the additional documentation that exist mentioned in this chapter.

There are three very well documented and authenticated historical documents that point to Paul having made the trip. These include: the Letter from Clement, Bishop of Rome in the year 96 AD; the Muratorian Fragment from the middle of the second century, and the Apocryphal Gospel of Peter, also from the middle of the second century. These will be presented in more detail here.

A. Evidence Supported by a Very Important Early Church Father: St. Clement, Third Bishop of Rome, His Letter to the Corinthians, 96 AD

Fig. 18: Pope Clement-I, Bishop of Rome 88 AD—99 AD[45]

The first of these is the testimony of Saint Clement-I, Bishop of Rome, in 96 AD.

In a letter from Pope Clement-I to the Church at Corinth, written in 96 AD, Clement clearly states that Paul had been in Hispania. This letter has been well preserved in Church archives, so it is highly authenticated. Church history indicates that Peter himself ordained Clement as a Church leader around the year 66 AD, and that he was the third successor of Peter as Bishop of Rome following Linus (some ancient chronological documents have Clement as Peter's fourth successor, with Cletus following Linus before Clement, while others have Cletus following Clement[46]).

It is therefore certain that Clement had to have been very much aware of Paul's activities for two reasons. The first is that in the year 66 AD, when Clement was ordained, Paul was well known to Roman Christians. Keep in mind that only two years before Paul had spent two years there in "house arrest" and during those two years he received visitors from the Christian community of Rome. It would be inconceivable that either Clement would not have visited him or that he would not have known of his presence in Rome. It is also important to document that Paul actually mentions a certain Clement as one of his companions in his letter to the Philippians, where he urges two members of the Philippian community to:

> "² I exhort Euodia and Syntyche to be of the same mind in the Lord. ³ I ask you also, true companions, help those women who labored with me in the gospel, with *Clement also*, and with my other fellow laborers, whose names are in the Book of Life."
> (Philippians 4: 2-3)

Clement later became Bishop of Rome in the year 88 AD, which was only 21 years after the date of Paul's estimated execution in the year 67 AD in Rome. That Clement had to have known of Paul's activities is a vital point because around the year 96 AD Clement wrote his letter addressed to the Christians in Corinth[47], which ranks as one of the earliest, if not the earliest, of surviving Christian documents along with the Didache[48]. In this first letter to the Corinthians, where Clement highlights the sacrifices of Peter and Paul, he said the following in verses 5: 6-7 about Paul[49]:

> "⁶ Seven times he was incarcerated and put in chains; he was exiled and stoned; heralded the word of Christ in the East and

in the West, projecting the noble renown of his faith. ⁷—And after teaching righteousness unto the whole world and having *reached the farthest bounds of the West;* and when he had borne his testimony before the rulers, he departed from the world and went unto the holy place, having been found a notable pattern of patient endurance." (CL 5:6-7)

By including the reference, "...the farthest bounds of the west," Clement makes a clear statement that Paul went to Hispania, since that was the common reference to Hispania in Roman times.

This personal testimony by St. Clement, well-documented in church archives, is a powerful assertion that Paul indeed visited Hispania. It is perhaps the strongest argument that many Church historians are now focusing on since he must have known of Paul's mission to Hispania. There is no doubt that this letter was written at the end of the reign of Emperor Domitian, who had launched yet another persecution of Christians that ended with his death in 96 AD.

Disproving Arguments Made by Some Historians Who Disagree with Clément's Assertion that Paul Made the Trip to Hispania
Clement's powerful assertion that Paul visited Hispania on a missionary trip comes from the earliest first-hand personal witness account of an "Apostolic Father of the Church[50]". It is baffling to read how some historians twist his testimony to disproof Paul's trip to Hispania. These historians claim that Clement was simply making reference to Paul's "intention" to go to Hispania based on Paul's letter to the Romans (15:22-29). They claim that because there are no writings that have survived from early churches in Hispania of Paul having been there, that it would be highly improbable that Paul made a missionary trip there. And yet, they ignore the argument that Clement must have been well aware of Paul's activities after the end of his house arrest.

The implication that Paul never made it to Hispania because there is a lack of documentation clearly ignores several historical facts. As already mentioned in the previous chapter, there were a number of brutal persecutions against Christians by the Romans and Muslims, where documents and relics were destroyed. We must also consider the customs and traditions of the Germanic Visigoth Christians that took over Hispania following the fall of the Roman Empire at the end of the fifth century. The Visigoths were originally northern Germanic tribes, so their Christian traditions would not have included references to Paul having preached in Hispania.

In fact, the Christianization of the Visigoths began with an effort by Roman emperor Constantius II in the mid-V century as Rome integrated those tribes into the Roman empire[51]. These Visigoth Christians were the ones that eventually settled in Hispania. Following the Muslim invasion of 711 AD, a group of these Christians that survived the invasion resettled in a small northern section of Hispania known as Asturias. It was from Asturias that the Visigoth Christians began the slow recovery of their Christian lands that took over 700 years. Because of the origins of their Christianization, they would have little, or no knowledge, that Paul had preached there several centuries before.

The same argument follows with regard to the Muslim invasion of Hispania from northern Africa, which began in 711 AD. By the year 722 AD, Muslims had taken all of Hispania with the exception of Asturias, controlled by the Visigoth Christians. During the first two centuries of Islamic occupation, Muslim invaders conducted a strategy of burning and destroying any documentation or reference to Christianity. They also executed Christians who would not subjugate to Muslim rule. This was part of the Muslim strategy, referred by some historians as "Shock and Terror" in order to keep Christian communities under control.[52]

It was not until 1248 AD, when King Fernando III, completed the slow, five-century effort by a line of Christian kings to recover their Christian lands (with the exception of Granada), that Christians were able to begin the process of fully reconstructing the Church in Hispania. Fernando III was a descendent of Visigoth Christian kings. We therefore ask the question, what would have been their Christian traditions at that point in history? The answer is clear. What survived were most likely the traditions of the Visigoth Christians, originally Germanic northern tribes who settled in Hispania between the years 500 AD and 711 AD.

Given that the Christian traditions that would have survived in Hispania were those of the Visigoth Christians, it is reasonable to conclude that many traditions of the early Hispanic Christian Church of the first century, which had Roman traditions, had been lost. The surviving Christians of the first couple of centuries of the second millennial AD, would have had little knowledge of Paul having been in Hispania 1000 years earlier since most of the documentation would have been destroyed or lost. From a historical research perspective, this conclusion should not be considered a simple hypothesis but a highly likely probability of what could have happened to the traditions that Paul had been in Hispania.

It is therefore important to consider evidence from other writings or sources from outside of Hispania to determine the likelihood Paul preached in Hispania.

This takes us back to the very strong assertion from Clement that Paul had been in Hispania. In this regard, it must be acknowledged that as an early Apostolic Father of the Church, one who must have personally known Paul, Clement's testimony should be given a very high level of credibility when making his assertion that Paul went to Hispania.

Thus, as we continue to expand on Paul's missionary trip to Spain, it is important to understand the very critical point laid out in this section: that the written testimony from Clement-I must absolutely be given the highest level of legitimacy and authenticity. This is one of the earliest authenticated writings in Church archives, written in

96 AD, by someone who was intimately familiar with Peter, since it was Peter who ordained him as presbyter of the Church of Rome. He must have also been, at the very least, personally aware of Paul if not intimately familiar with him since Paul spent two years in house-arrest in Rome preaching the Word of Christ to everyone who visited him. It would be illogical to think that Clement would not have visited him, or at least known of his activities after Paul was set free. It would therefore be irresponsible to discount Clement's writing as some historians have done.

The fact that Clement clearly indicated Paul travelled to Hispania must therefore be seriously considered as a fact, and only challenged with undeniable evidence to the contrary. That undeniable evidence does not exist.

B. The Muratorian Fragment

This fragment is a copy of what is considered to be the oldest known references of the books of the New Testament (see Fig. 19 below for a picture of the fragment). It is a 7th-century manuscript in Latin, bound in a 7th or 8th century codex consisting of 85 lines of text. It was originally kept in the library of the Columbanus' monastery at the Bobbio Abbey in Italy.

The abbey was founded by Saint Columbanus in the year 614 AD, and over the years stored a number of early Christian writings and documents from antiquity[53]. The Muratorian fragment was later moved to the Ambrosian Library in Milan where it remained until it was discovered by biblical historian Father Ludovico Antonio Muratori (1672–1750). The fragment contains elements that indicate it is a translation from a Greek original, written between 160 to 170 AD. It is a portion of what remains from a larger document, whose author has remained unknown. It lists most of the writings accepted by the early Church as canonical, that is, official works inspired by God. Father Muratori published his findings in 1740[54].

Fig. 19: Rough Image of the Muratorian Fragment, written in Latin[55]

In this document, the original author includes a very important reference in relation to Luke as the author of the Acts of the Apostles, and clearly references Paul having made the trip to Hispania. In verses 34-39 the fragment's author writes:

"... (34) Moreover, the acts of all the apostles (35) were written in one book. For 'most excellent Theophilus' Luke compiled (36) the individual events that took place in his presence — (37) as he plainly shows by omitting the martyrdom of Peter (38) as well as the departure of Paul from the city [of Rome] (39) when he journeyed to Hispania....." (Muratorian Canon, 34-39[56])

What can we conclude from this statement? Its author clearly implies that St. Luke, who wrote the Gospel According to Luke as well as the Acts of the Apostles, had to have known of Paul's trip to Hispania but did not include it in Acts of the Apostles because Luke did not personally witness it. This would indicate two important points:

1) It was common knowledge to the author, as well as to Christian communities during the years 160-170, that Paul had been on a missionary trip to Hispania, and that Luke, at the time he wrote

Acts, must have also considered it common knowledge, therefore, there was no need to include that information in Acts of the Apostles; and,

2) That Luke, knowing it was common knowledge to the early Christian communities, purposely did not include that information in Acts.

Why would Luke not include the trip to Hispania as a continuation to Acts? The author of the Muratorian Fragment clearly states that Paul "... journeyed to Hispania." This document was written between the years 160-170 AD, so it was common knowledge to early Christian communities that Paul's missionary trip to Hispania took place.

Surely, Luke had to have known this and yet he purposely did not include it in Acts of the apostles. Why?

As has already been mentioned in the previous chapter, perhaps Luke planned to include Paul's trip in a later writing that has either, never been found, or that Luke simply didn't have a chance to write. Either of these possibilities are in line with the realities of what was taking place during the time Luke would have written Acts.

The fact remains that the abrupt end to Acts has been the subject of much discussion by historians over the centuries. This possibility of Paul having made the trip could even explain why Luke would have wanted to start a whole new book, since that would focus on Paul alone, and in it, include the results of his being set free. He could have also wanted to wait for Paul to have written a letter/epistle himself to the Hispaniards, but as we have already explained, Paul never got a chance to write that epistle. That is why this reference in the Muratorian fragment is so intriguing since it clearly indicates that it was common knowledge in the second century that Paul travelled to Hispania, and just as important, that Luke must have had knowledge of the trip but did not include it in Acts of the Apostles.

Another compelling point made in the fragment is the reference that the martyrdom of Peter was not included in Acts by Luke since he did not personally witness it. Again, this would indicate that at the time Acts was written, Luke and the Christian community had ample knowledge of Peter's execution, and yet Luke did not include it as an additional element in Acts. Perhaps Luke had other plans to write a separate book about Paul and Peter, but he never had a chance to do so, or as could easily be the case with ancient texts, he wrote the book, but it has never been found.

There is some controversy on exactly what year the original document represented by the Muratorian fragment was written. Some historians have it as coming from the fourth century, which is later than the estimated 160-170 AD by most historians[57]. Either way, the important point here is that it provides a perspective of what the very early community of Christians believed to be common knowledge. So again, having, a) the well-documented testimony from St. Clement, and, b) this fragment expressing what the early Christian community took as common knowledge, is a powerful combination of documents that support the fact Paul visited Hispania.

We continue in the next section with the very compelling Apocryphal Acts of Peter, which also provides passages that Paul did indeed make the trip to Hispania.

C. Apocryphal Acts of Peter

The Acts of Peter, written in Greek, is one of the earliest of the apocryphal books and documents. Biblical historians believe it was written in Asia Minor around 150 AD by a disciple of one of Peter's disciples, towards the end of that disciple's life[58].

It is important to here explain what these apocryphal books were and why they are important in the context of the research being presented in this book. These were early writings about the life of Jesus and the apostles that have been dated to sometime in the second century. About fifty of these books have been found and they fall mostly into two categories. The first is the category of "heretical," because they were written to support a position found to be heresy by the early Church and continue to be designated as such today.

The second category is "legendary," written to provide additional information to the accepted canonical gospels based on oral legends that began during those first two centuries. Books in this second "legendary" category contain important historical information that the Church has concluded is historically accurate; however, they have not been included in the New Testament because they were not written by a direct witness to Jesus or the Apostles, or were identified as not being inspired by the Holy Spirit. The Gospel of Peter falls into this second category[59].

A major challenge for biblical historians is how to take these apocryphal writings into consideration since even the authors of the "legendary" writings have never been confirmed. The early Church of the first five centuries decided to accept those "legendary" writings and use them as historical references since they contained historical information that has been verified by other sources. Those that could not be verified historically or contained "heretical" writings have not been accepted. Nonetheless, these "legendary" early apocryphal writings provide an important perspective on the life of Jesus and the actions taken by the Apostles after their deaths.

It should be noted that it took until the fifth century and various ecumenical councils to arrive at what were considered "canonical" books that comprised the New Testament. These early councils established the requirement that for books to be included in the New Testament they had to have been written by an author that could provide direct personal testimony of Jesus' or the apostles' lives and actions[60].

Furthermore, it was not until the year 1546, during the Council of Trent, that the Roman Catholic Church provided its first dogmatic definition of the Church's entire canon. This put a stop to doubts and disagreements about the status of the apocryphal books since they had continued to be studied and quoted by various Christian groups dating from the beginning of the Church[61].

The Acts of Peter is therefore one of the first legendary-apocryphal books that fits into the category of a book that provides a significant amount of historical information and perspective. Its text has survived only in the Latin translation of the Vercelli Manuscript, the Codex Vercellensis Evangeliorum preserved since the late fourth century in the cathedral library of Vercelli, in Italy, under the title *Actus Petri cum Simone*.[62] It was composed in Greek, and as mentioned before, was believed to have been written in the second century, somewhere in Asia Minor, by a disciple of one of Peter's disciples. It provides the first written record of the Catholic Church's tradition that St. Peter was crucified head-down, which was considered common knowledge by the second century, and has continued through today's Church tradition.

The reference to Peter being crucified upside down is given in Ch. 36, 7-9 of the apocryphal Acts of Peter. This reference is being included here because it confirms that the Acts of Peter has been used by the Church over the years as a document with authenticated legendary information.

If the Acts of Peter is considered authenticated by the Church in regard to Peter's martyrdom, then the references found in it to Paul's trip to Hispania should also be considered authenticated.

If we first examine Peter's execution and martyrdom, the Acts of Peter states that Peter addressed his executioners with the following statement, referring first to himself and then speaking to the executioners:

> "But it is time for you, Peter, to surrender your body to those who are taking it ... Take it, then, you whose duty it is. I request you therefore, executioners, to crucify me head-downwards in this way and no other." [63]

It's important to note that this is the written documentation that the Church has used throughout its history, in addition to oral tradition, as the reference that Peter was crucified head-down. It provides a historical assertion of Peter's execution.

In Acts of Peter, a very definitive statement was also included in Chapter-3:1, about Christ's instructions for Paul to go to Hispania:

> "He [Paul] fasted for three days, and Paul prayed to our Lord to show him what he should do next, and he then saw a vision in which the Lord said to him: 'Arise, Paul, and become a physician in thy body (by going thither in person) to them that are in Hispania.' ..."[64]

In addition to this passage, the Acts of Peter also provides a definitive statement of Paul having been in Hispania by including a passage about the Christian community of Rome going to greet him after he returned from Hispania. This passage in particular should be taken as a very important testimonial from early Christianity:

> "Having returned to Rome, Saint Paul coming from the Hispanias, all the Christians went out to meet him ...".[65]

Given the large population of gentiles in Hispania, and the word of mouth dissemination of Paul's accomplishments, this is a strong reference likely made by one of Peter's close disciples to the author of the Acts of Peter. Keep in mind that the author was himself a later disciple of Peter's disciple. The important reference here is that it was well known in early Church history that members of the Christian community of Rome went out to greet Paul upon his return to Rome from Hispania. We could also surmise from historical accounts, that given Nero's brutal persecution of Christians, members of the community perhaps went out to warn Paul of the evolving persecution.

Most historians believe the Acts of Peter was written 70-90 years after Paul's execution. The author must have been a dedicated disciple of a very disciplined disciple of Peter since biblical historians have cited significant references in this book that have a high level of historical credibility. Being so close to the time that Peter was alive and getting the information from someone who was likely a living witness and follower of Peter, makes the documentation provided in the book very credible.

The crucial point here is that there are important references in the Acts of Peter that Paul went to Hispania. This has led some historians to believe that it was a fairly well-established fact in the early Christian communities that Paul travelled to Hispania.

When we combine the Acts of Peter, with the letter to the Corinthians by Clement, who was the third Bishop of Rome and must have known Paul personally when he made the definitive statement in his letter to the Corinthians that Paul made the trip, and further add the clear implication in the Muratorian Fragment that Paul made the trip, we have very strong documentation that Paul indeed made the trip.

We continue by providing very compelling additional evidence in the coming chapter from six "Doctors of the Church."

CHAPTER 4

THE WRITINGS FROM SIX OTHER EARLY "DOCTORS" OF THE CHURCH

As mentioned in the previous chapter, the powerful testimony from St. Clement, along with the reference in the Muratorian fragment that the early Christian community knew of Paul's trip to Hispania, provide two very credible testimonies of Paul's trip. I then added the direct references that Paul travelled to Hispania found in the Apocryphal Acts of Peter.

These is a very strong set of documented and authenticated references from early Christian communities confirming Paul made the trip. When you add them to the previous biblical references presented in Chapter-2 that also clearly implied Paul made the trip, it starts to become really hard to contradict all of these references.

By themselves, these references should be convincing enough to allow any biblical scholar to conclude Paul made the trip. For sure, many historians have made definitive conclusions on other history elements with less evidence than what has been presented here so far.

But there's much more. We have the writings of six early Church "Fathers", also recognized as "Doctors of the Church," listed chronologically in this chapter, that also make either a direct or an indirect reference to Paul's missionary trip to Hispania. These Doctors of the Church were from what today we refer to the Eastern Orthodox Churches, many of which were founded by Paul. These churches all had very close connections to the Christian Church of Jerusalem, so their knowledge of the missionary trips of the Apostles should have been very deep, especially of Paul's trips since he was instrumental in the founding of many of these churches.

It would therefore be illogical to think that Church leaders from these churches did not have a very detailed history of the missionary trips carried out by the Apostles and later disciples. Unfortunately, a large part of whatever written historical Christian records that existed at the time were destroyed and lost after these regions were first conquered by the Persians and later by the Arab Muslims.

This is exactly what happened to the City of Alexandria, which was first captured by the Persian King Khosrau in the year 616 AD, and only a short time later, by the Arab Muslims in the year 641 AD. There are numerous historical accounts that the Christian Churches at the time tried to move whatever relics they had to regions they felt were much safer. The Bishop of Alexandria, for example, moved a crate full of relics to Hispania. Three centuries later, when this crate was finally opened under the supervision of the Bishop of Oviedo (Asturias, northern Spain), the famous Sudarium of Oviedo, the cloth used to cover the face of Christ at burial, was found.

So, fortunately, some of the writings of homilies and letters from Christian leaders throughout this region were saved in one way or another and moved to different locations for safekeeping. These writings, together with the evidence presented in the previous chapters, provide an overwhelming amount of documented positive references to Paul making the trip.

The evidence being presented in this book, therefore, continues to establish an incontrovertible set of arguments that are hard to refute.

We begin the writings with the highly distinguished Saint Athanasius, Bishop of Alexandria.

A. Saint Athanasius, Bishop of Alexandria between 328 and 373AD

Fig. 20: Athanásios Alexandrías; also called Athanasius the Apostolic, primarily in the Coptic Orthodox Church, was the twentieth bishop of Alexandria (as Athanasius I). Declared "Doctor of the Church" by the Vatican and Eastern Orthodox Churches

Saint Athanasius[66] was a highly respected early leader of the Christian church, who later received the designation of "Doctor of the Church" for his teachings and writings on Christian life. He was the Bishop during the fourth century of Alexandria, a city which was known as perhaps the most important center of the Hellenistic civilization period, in which there were major advances in philosophy and the sciences. Given its relatively close geographic proximity to Jerusalem, it was also one of the largest urban centers for Jewish communities of that time.

Because of its close connection to the Christian Church of Jerusalem, and the fact Alexandria was a center that allowed for the keeping of historical records, it is logical to conclude leaders of that

Church had a deep knowledge of Apostolic missionary trips. Church tradition has it that Christianity was founded in Alexandria before the year 40 AD by the Evangelist Mark, who was one of Peter's closest disciples. Because of the relative tolerance that existed there, the Church grew to become an important early center of Christianity.

In one of his writings on the commitment to the Church by its members, he wrote the following concerning Paul's missionary works, including a reference to his visit to Hispania:

> *"... For these reasons, and his saintly fervor to preach to the eastern limits of Illyricum, he marched with no hesitation to Rome and later embarked to Hispania, working to his limits in order to reach his highest rewards."*[67]

Here we have a clear assertion in the mid-fourth century by the highly respected Church Father, St. Athanasius, a church historian himself, at a time not so distant from Paul's death, confirming Paul did make his desired trip. Historians who refuse to acknowledge that Paul visited Hispania argue that Athanasius was merely recounting what Paul had said in his letter to the Romans. That goes contrary to the much more likely scenario that Athanasius, a Bishop from a city that prided itself on maintaining historical documentations, and from one of the regions where Paul founded several churches, would have been very aware of Paul's missionary trips. He and others from the Church of Alexandria were removed by less than 300 years from Paul's missionary trips. It is much more logical to think that at the time of St. Athanasius church tradition would still be fairly accurate and not distorted. This would give his assertion a high level of credibility that should not be easily discarded.

B. Saint Cyril, Bishop of Jerusalem from 350 to 386AD[68]

Fig. 21: Saint Cyril; c. 313-386 AD. Bishop of Jerusalem. He is venerated as a saint by the Roman Catholic Church, the Eastern Orthodox Church, and the Anglican Communion. Declared Doctor of the Church by the Vatican and Orthodox churches

St. Cyril was a distinguished theologian who was also declared Doctor of the Church by the Vatican.[69] He is highly respected by the Eastern Orthodox Church, the Roman Catholic Church, and the Palestinian Christian Community. In one of his catechist writings he wrote the following reference regarding Paul's missionary trips to all corners of the world:

> "... he [Paul] spread the Gospel from Jerusalem to Illyricum, even evangelizing in Imperial Rome, and extending into Hispania in his desire to preach the Word of Jesus, undergoing innumerable conflicts and performing signs and wonders."[70]

St. Cyril wrote this passage during the time he was Bishop of Jerusalem. The early church in Jerusalem must have been aware that Paul's extensive missionary trips included Hispania. If Paul had not made the trip to Hispania, you would think that the early Church of Jerusalem would have known exactly what happened to him. It would be illogical to think that if instead he would have been either tried in "Imperial Rome" and executed at the end of his first imprisonment, or returned to Jerusalem after he was set free, the Church of Jerusalem would have known. Instead, Cyril makes the definitive statement that Paul "extended" the Gospel to Hispania.

Therefore, although Cyril does not expressly state that Paul was in Hispania, his reference implies that this was a well-known fact in the early Christian communities, including the community of Jerusalem. If Paul had not made this trip, early Churches and their leaders would have known he never made it. And yet, here is another indication that he did make it.

C. Saint John Chrysostom, Archbishop of Constantinople from 397 to 407AD

Fig. 22: Saint John Chrysostom (349-407AD) Declared Doctor of the Church by the Vatican and Eastern Orthodox Churches; Archbishop of Constantinople from 397 to 407AD

St. John Chrysostom was an important early Church leader, declared Doctor of the Church for his deep understanding of Scripture and his related writings. In Antioch, where he was ordained a deacon in 381AD, St. John became known for his homilies and his insightful analysis of Bible passages. As the Archbishop from the region of Antioch, where Paul spent a significant amount of time, he and his Church community must have been very aware of the true and factual travels of Paul before he was executed in Rome.

In one of his homilies analyzing 2 Timothy 4: 6, St. John makes a very astute conclusion based on Paul's comments to Timothy, a conclusion we already mentioned in Chapter-2 but repeat here given that this reference comes directly from St. John.

In 2 Timothy 4:6, Paul writes: "⁶For I am already being poured out like a drink offering, and the time for my departure is near. ⁷I have fought the good fight, I have finished the race."

St. John interprets this passage as Paul completing what was one of his highest priorities towards the end of his missionary life, that of evangelizing the gentiles in Hispania. To this point, St. John concludes his homily saying that, *"After having been in Rome, he [Paul] traveled to Hispania ... "*.[71]

But perhaps much more definitive was St. John's statement to his congregation in another homily in the year 387AD addressing Christians that were participating in Hebrew festivals, where he made the following reference about Paul[72]:

"He was imprisoned two years in Rome; afterwards he was placed in liberty. He then went to Hispania, and later to Judea where he visited the Jews. He then went again to Rome, where he perished under Nero."

Here we have another Doctor of the Church and distinguished Church historian, who in the early years of Christianity, prior to the year 400, writes definitively of Paul's trip to Hispania. Perhaps more important, there is no hesitation in his reference to Paul's visit to Hispania in at least two of his important writings.

These assertions by St. John are so direct that they can't be dismissed and must be given the highest level of credibility, especially as more references are added by early Doctors of the Church to Paul having traveled to Hispania.

I have also reached the same conclusions using my own analysis and must therefore concur with the assertion made by St. John.

D. Saint Jerome (Jeronimo Eusebius Sophronius Hieronymus, 347-420AD)

Fig. 23: Saint Jeronimo Eusebius Sophronius Hieronymus; (347-420AD). Declared Doctor of the Church by the Vatican and Eastern Orthodox Churches

St. Jerome was another highly respected theologian and biblical historian who received the designation of Doctor of the Church for his writings on the moral conduct of Christians. He wrote the following concerning Paul being freed by Nero, and later traveling to Hispania:

> *"Paul was freed from imprisonment by Nero and this allowed him to preach the Gospel of Christ in the western regions, as he attests in his second letter to Timothy written while he was again in jail, from where he writes his letter..."*[73]

Saint Jerome also added in a separate text the following:

> *"Paul, called by the Lord, travelled all over the world to spread the Gospel, from Jerusalem to the province of Illyricum, to not build on top of where others had already preached, and extended the Word to Hispania from the Red Sea, in fact, from ocean to ocean"*[74]

Again, here is another Doctor of the Church, around the year 400 AD clearly expressing his understanding that Paul did extend his missionary trip to Hispania.

But St. Jerome makes two important observations in the quotes above that must be analyzed carefully. In the first quote he clearly states that Paul *was freed by Nero from his first imprisonment in Rome*, which again asserts that Paul was set free after his two years in a Roman prison. This is an important point because many historians still question whether he was freed after his two years in prison. St. Jerome is clear, however, that Paul was freed the first time, and then confirms that the *second letter to Timothy was written during Paul's second time in a Roman jail.*

These two points are very important assertions by someone who was declared a Father of the Church and was only 300 years removed from the time Paul completed his missionary trips. He must have been well informed of verified and documented information on Paul's trips.

St. Jerome also states that Paul was able to preach in the "western regions," which from the perspective of being in Rome, the western regions included France, Britain, and Hispania. It was normal practice in Roman times to refer to Hispania as the "westernmost" region of the Empire and when a statement was made about the western, or westernmost, region, the reference was almost universally of Hispania. In any case, in his second quote above, St. Jerome clearly states that Paul "... *extended the Word to Hispania from the Red Sea, in fact, from ocean to ocean."* This statement leaves little doubt that he was able to preach in Hispania.

There is an additional very important observation by St. Jerome that must not be taken lightly when he connects Paul's *Second Letter to Timothy* to the assertion that Paul preached in the westernmost regions. Although Paul does not state directly that he traveled to the western regions, St. Jerome concludes that Paul's testimony to Timothy that he was able "... to finish the race ...." leaves no doubt that finishing the race meant he was able to go to Hispania.

Many historians, including myself, and in this case also St. Jerome, have reached the same conclusion that this testimony by Paul to

Timothy meant he had been to Hispania. Why? Because Timothy was very aware of Paul's plans to preach to gentiles, and in particular, of his plan to preach in Hispania. In the context in which the letter was written, telling Timothy that he had finished the race can only be interpreted as a direct indication he had to have traveled there.

E. St. Epiphanius of Salamis, Bishop of Cyprus from 365 to 403

Fig. 24: Saint Epiphanius, c. 310/320 to 403, was bishop of Salamis, Cyprus at the end of the 4th century. He was declared a saint and Doctor of the Church by both the Vatican and Eastern Orthodox.

St. Epiphanius was known for maintaining a strict orthodox interpretation of scriptures.

He was one of the first to take up the matter of veneration of Christian images. He was also declared Doctor of the Church.

In one of his writings around the year 400, St. Epiphanius includes a very simple statement[75]: *"Paul was able to reach Hispania, and Peter travelled frequently to Ponto and Bitinia."*

In this particular writing, St. Epiphanius makes this statement as a matter of fact, without any allusion of there being any doubt that Paul was able to make the trip. This again is another assertion by another early Doctor of the Church having the understanding that Paul traveled to Spain.

As these assertions by early Church leaders continue to mount, notice that these are coming from outside of Hispania. The reason for this has already been mentioned in the previous section. Hardly any documents or books survived the brutal 300 years of persecutions by Romans and later the ruthless persecutions of Christians during the first 300-years of Muslims occupation of Hispania after their invasion of 711 AD.

F. St. Theodoret of Cyrus, Bishop of Cyrus 423 to 457 [76]

Fig. 25: St. Theodoret

To finish this section on Church historians' testimony we add a sixth Father of the Church, St. Theodoret, an influential theologian of the School of Antioch and a highly respected biblical historian. Theodoret played a controversial and pivotal role in several 5th-century, Byzantine Church controversies that led to various ecumenical acts and schisms. He is called "blessed" in the Eastern Orthodox Church, and some Chalcedonian and East Syrian Christian Churches regard him as a saint.

Although Theodoret was a controversial figure, he nonetheless was a highly respected biblical historian, which is why his assertion that Paul travelled to Hispania is so important. Theodoret made one of the most definitive statements in early Christianity of Paul having traveled to Hispania[77]:

> "... Paul first escaped the ire of Nero, as he explained in his second letter to Timothy (2 Tim 4, 16-17). The writings of Acts of the Apostles tell us that he was in Rome for two years, staying in his

rented house, and from there he left for Hispania, preaching the divine Gospel to people there; he returned, and was beheaded."

This is such a definitive statement, made by an early Christian historian and theologian, considered a well-informed scholar of Christian history, that we cannot dismiss it as somehow being misinformed. Perhaps even more important, he was one of the most distinguished historians from the School of Antioch, a region where Paul spent a significant amount of time preaching. How could he not be totally aware and knowledgeable of the true and factual missionary trips of Paul?

G. Personal Insights derived from the writings of these six early Christian Church Fathers

In my research of Historians that disagree with the premise that Paul traveled to Hispania, I find that they either make no mention, or make very scant mentions, of the references included in this chapter.

The references in this chapter are all from early Christian leaders of the first four centuries, all of them biblical historians and distinguished theologians, designated "Doctors of the Church" precisely because of their knowledge of Christianity. We can only conclude that those that disagree with the fact Paul travelled to Hispania are either ignorant of these references or tend to discount them as somehow not being clear or direct enough.

These disagreeing historians might make references to one or two of the above Church fathers but do not mention the compilation of the six mentioned here. Many also tend to ignore that Clement-I must have known Paul, and his letter to the Corinthians, written within 30 years of Paul's execution, clearly states Paul travelled to Hispania.

These disagreeing historians also ignore the fact that the early Doctors of the Church referenced in this chapter had to have had access to much more personal information and eyewitness accounts of Paul's missionary trips. Keep in mind that there must have been many other early Christian writings that have not survived over the ages. These could easily have included Paul's trip to Hispania, and those written accounts could simply have been lost with the passage of time or were just not written down.

Therefore, considering that many ancient writings never survived, we have to give the ones referenced in this chapter, from six distinguished Church Fathers, the highest level of credibility and legitimacy. In fact, since they are from the first four centuries of the Church's history, we should use them as a very definitive element in our conclusion that Paul did travel to Hispania.

CHAPTER 5

DOCUMENTING THE STRONG ORAL TRADITION OF EASTERN ORTHODOX CHURCHES AS WELL AS CITIES IN SPAIN THAT PAUL MADE THE TRIP

As I continued to expand my research on the premise that Paul visited Hispania on a missionary trip, one piece of evidence after another kept popping up that supported this premise. I have identified so much information on Paul's trip to Hispania that when we apply a scientific research process it becomes difficult for anyone to refute it. In fact, I have yet to find in other research writings on Paul's travels some of the evidence that's being presented in this book. I have found evidence that directly and indirectly supports this premise, including maps and local oral traditions. But when you connect all of this evidence, the preponderance of the evidence allows for reaching an unrefutably strong set of conclusions.

In this chapter we will cover the oral traditions that exists that Paul made the trip to Hispania. This includes some very strong oral traditions that have been handed down through Christianity ever since the Early Church was established.

Before presenting that oral tradition, it is important to first take a moment and recap how this research project started and where this research has led us to this point.

This has been a ten-year research project, that as mentioned in the Prologue section at the start of the book, began during a last-minute weekend visit to the city of Ecija (Spain) planned by my wife, Celi. She had heard that there were many beautiful churches and church-towers in the city, which was known as the City of Towers. Since she had wanted to go there for some time, and since it was only an hour from the City of Seville, where I was completing my doctoral dissertation at the University of Seville, she wanted to explore the city that weekend.

As I mentioned in the Prologue section, at Mass that Sunday in Ecija, the priest included the strong oral tradition in his homily that back in the first century AD, during apostolic times, the Apostle Paul preached in Ecija. The priest then mentioned that before leaving Ecija, Paul promised the followers he had converted, that he would return some day. The priest continued and brought up the miracle in 1436 that had been attributed to Paul, fulfilling the promise that he would be returning to Ecija. Ever since that miracle took place in 1436, every year there is a special celebration with processions throughout the city to commemorate Paul's visit in the first century. This miracle is detailed later in this chapter.

Before Mass that Sunday in Ecija, I had never heard of Paul having been in Spain, or Hispania as it was then called. I was so intrigued by what the priest had said, that when I returned to my home town of Miami, I began to research whether there was a possibility that Paul had been in Spain, and in particular in Ecija.

Fig. 26: A St. Paul's procession celebrated through the streets of Ecija[78]

To my surprise, right from the beginning all types of direct and indirect evidence started to come out that supported the premise Hispania had been his last missionary trip before he returned to Rome where he was quickly arrested and executed.

I started to wonder: why has Paul's trip to Spain never been given more exposure? Why hasn't the Church, especially the Church in Spain, not raised awareness of his potential trip and done a more complete, in-depth analysis of that possibility? The answer to these questions will become clearer in the final chapter where conclusions on this research project will be presented.

In Chapter-2 a pretty compelling set of biblical writings were provided to support Paul made the trip, although admittedly, as strong as the indications were these writings did not provide direct evidence. This was followed in Chapter-3 by three authenticated documents that began to establish the proof needed to confirm that Paul made the trip. These were: first, the letter to the Corinthians in 96 AD from Clement-1 Bishop of Rome, in which he mentions directly that Paul went to Hispania; second, the Muratorian Fragment from around the year 150 AD clearly implying Paul made the trip; and third, the historically authenticated Apocryphal Acts of Peter, also from around the year 150 AD in which several direct references were made to Paul having gone to Hispania.

In Chapter-4, the writings were then presented from six different early Doctors of the Church, all being biblical historians themselves, which documented that Paul made the trip.

How can all of these very strong pieces of evidence be possibly ignored? All of them come from separate sources, but all of them support Paul's missionary trip to Hispania. Can we add any additional evidence to these historical and biblical references?

Well, my research found several oral traditions that are also so strong it would be illogical to ignore them altogether. Keep in mind that many Church positions as well as general conclusions reached throughout history are based on oral traditions. I, therefore, present those oral traditions in this chapter in order to further support the findings and evidence that Paul travelled to Hispania.

A. The Oral Tradition from the Eastern Orthodox Churches

One day, in the middle of this research project, I ran into a long-time friend of mine with whom I had worked during my corporate years. I had only spoken to him sporadically during the past ten years, but this time we had time to sit down and have a nice cup of coffee.

Knowing that he was a very devout Christian, we started speaking about our Christian faith and the pressures in society to try to reduce its importance. I had forgotten that his family actually followed the Eastern Orthodox Christian rites, and so he gave me a pleasant surprise when he informed me that he had become a Priest in the Antiochian Orthodox Christian Church. In fact, he had just been confirmed as the Interim Pastor of Saint Philip Orthodox Christian Church in South Florida.

I then mentioned the research I was conducting, and he became very intrigued with my findings dealing with the Apostle Paul's travels to Hispania. He proceeded to tell me that in the Eastern Orthodox churches, Paul's last missionary trip to Hispania is taken as a historical fact.

I was stunned. Why would the Eastern Orthodox churches have Paul's trip to Hispania as a fact, but the Roman Catholic church only acknowledges the possibility? He then followed up by providing me some old magazines he had received from Greek churches that mentioned Paul's trip to Hispania.

To further support that this oral tradition was taken as a fact in the Eastern Churches, my friend later coordinated a conference call with a well-known Antiochian Orthodox Church biblical historian who is also a priest. This historian proceeded to confirm that although written evidence has never surfaced, it is a well-established oral tradition in the Eastern Churches that Paul did visit Hispania on a missionary trip.

After speaking with my friend and with the priest historian, it dawned on me that the six Doctors of the Church mentioned in Chapter-4 all came from the Eastern Christian churches. These churches broke away from the Roman Catholic Church in the famous schism of the year 1054 AD. Known as the East-West schism in Christian history, one of the main causes of this schism was the rejection by the eastern churches that the primacy and theological directions of the Church had to come from the Bishop of Rome.

As will be explained in more detail in Chapter-6, this highly controversial issue actually began in the fourth century and was further exacerbated towards the end of the fifth century by Gelasius-I, Bishop of Rome. Around the year 496 AD, Gelasius, who was a biblical historian himself, began to aggressively advocate for the premise that the direct line of Peter as Bishop of Rome and Vicar of Christ, should hold the mantle of primacy of the Church.

Gelasius' strong position began to be accepted by other bishops under the Roman patriarchy and adopted by subsequent Bishops of Rome in the centuries that followed.

In one of Gelasius' writings, he discounted Paul's trip to Hispania, despite the overwhelming amount of evidence up to this point in Church history that he did make the trip. Gelasius, therefore, had a direct impact on the discussion of why Paul might not have been given the recognition that he conducted a missionary trip to Hispania.

This has led to the Roman Catholic Church taking a much more cautious position, acknowledging only the possibility of his trip. The controversy raised by Gelasius is such an important point that I have dedicated Chapter-6 to fully cover his controversial position.

It is, however, a very important consideration when discussing Paul's last missionary trip to Hispania to recognize that in the Eastern Orthodox Churches his trip is taken as a historical fact. We wonder what would have happened had the East-West schism not taken place. Would the accepted oral tradition from the Eastern churches that Paul did make the trip have remained?

For now, we continue in the next section with the documentation of additional oral traditions from within Hispania that would indicate Paul was able to travel to Hispania.

B. Oral Traditions from Within Spain that Paul Preached in Hispania

Historians are often faced with the issue of how to take into consideration oral traditions, passed down by word-of-mouth, to connect them to actual written or physical evidence that might exist. In the case of Paul's missionary trip to Hispania, there are several very strong oral traditions that must be analyzed that support the premise that he made trip.

We have already mentioned the oral tradition that exists in Tarragona that he entered Hispania through Tarraco, today's Tarragona. Tarraco was the Imperial Capital of the Province of Tarraconensis, with a large population during Paul's time. This oral tradition, strongly maintained in Tarragona, makes logical sense if Paul did in fact travel to Hispania. As the imperial capital, Tarraco was the shortest and normal entry point into Hispania for all ships coming from Rome. It would have certainly been where Paul would have entered.

In addition, there is evidence that in Tarraco at that time there was a Jewish community in existence. This is an important fact since Paul would have become aware of its existence during the two years in house-arrest in Rome, where he surely spent time planning his trip. Paul's normal practice was to visit large population areas with Jewish communities, and then begin by asking permission to speak in its synagogue. The fact a Jewish community existed there would have been an attractive point for Paul's initial entry into Hispania.

Having such a strong oral tradition in today's Tarragona that Paul preached there has to be given the highest consideration. I have personally interviewed the Director of the Biblical Museum of Tarragona, as well as the Archbishop of Tarragona and several other biblical historians there, and they are convinced that the oral tradition is accurate.

There is also another very strong tradition, mentioned at the beginning of this chapter, that Paul was in Astigi (today's Ecija), a thriving commercial center only 55 kilometers southwest of the Roman city Corduba (today's Cordoba). Corduba at the time was the important Capital of the Baetica Province, allowing for a close geographic and commercial relationship with Astigi. During Paul's time, Astigi was the administrative center of one of the four government districts of the Baetica Province, with Corduba as the overall capital of the Province. As such, Astigi was a thriving center for trade and commerce.

The very strong ancient oral tradition that is still embedded in the people of Astigi, states that while Paul was travelling through the Baetica province, he stopped in Astigi to preach to its residents. He would have been aware that there had been early Jewish communities in both Corduba and Astigi and this would have prompted Paul to visit the city. The fact there is very strong evidence that there were several very early Christian communities established in and around

Corduba and Astigi would indicate a very intense missionary effort took place there very early in Christianity.

The very strong ancient oral tradition from Astigi proclaims that around the years 64-65AD, Paul passed through Corduba and moved on to Astigi, where oral tradition states he preached next to a Roman temple situated by the Roman forum. There, tradition states that several government officials as well as community leaders stopped to listen and were eventually converted to Christianity. As part of the tradition, Paul promised before he left the town that he would return some day. With the growth of the early Christian communities, the oral tradition of Paul having been there was maintained for several centuries and that led to Paul being named Patron Saint of Astigi as far back as the VII century.

Even after the Muslim invasion in the year 711 AD, the oral tradition of Paul having been in Astigi was so strong, that it was passed down by families that secretly maintained their Christian beliefs during the 500-year Muslim presence in the Islamic caliphate of Al Andalus (756-1248 AD). After King Fernando III recovered Corduba and most of Al Andalus for Christianity in 1248, he became aware of the tradition and again encouraged the veneration of St. Paul in what now was being renamed as Ecija.

This tradition eventually led to what is today recognized in Ecija as the "Miracle of St. Paul," when in the year 1436, Paul appeared to Anton de Arjona, a humble 14-year-old peasant in a field outside of Ecija. After introducing himself as the Apostle Paul who had returned as promised, he instructed Anton to tell the officials in Ecija that they had been ignoring his original teachings. They needed to stop their sinful ways, or he would send a dreadful plague upon the city. Paul told Anton that all residents of the city would need to participate in a procession to the St. Paul and St. Domingo convent, and participate in a solemn Mass and ask for forgiveness. In order to make Anton a credible messenger and ensure he delivered the message, he knotted the young man's right hand into a stump and told him that it would be untied after the procession was completed.

Anton frightfully went to explain what happened to the government leaders of Ecija, and seeing what happened to Anton's hand, they believed the young man. They proceeded to conduct the procession as he explained, after which Anton's hand was cured right in front of the citizens present in the procession. In commemoration to this event, the government leaders vowed to continue this celebration every year, and this has continued non-stop ever since then.

It is precisely this non-stop yearly tradition in Ecija, with the well-documented miracle chronicled by the Bishop of Ecija in 1436, that carries so much weight in Church archives. In fact, the original documents from the year 1436 still exists, and untold conversions and healings from those participating in the processions have been documented.

There's also another oral tradition that dates back to the first century in the city of Italica, also in the Baetica Province, located only ten kilometers from the City of Hispalis, today's Seville. Italica was composed of mostly retired Roman legionnaires and reached a population of over 50,000 by the end of the first century. Documentation exists that Italica had been constituted into a Christian diocese by the end of the first century during Apostolic times. There's an ancient oral tradition whose source is not known, that by the last decade of the first century Italica had a bishop by the name of Gerontius, who was martyred in the year 100 AD.

According to a historical reference documented in the Catholic Encyclopedia, Gerontius was a disciple of one of the Apostles[79]. This reference provides an intriguing clue to the fact Paul was in Italica. Why? From Paul's own letters as well as Acts of the Apostle, we know that every time he came across a community willing to listen to the Word of Jesus, Paul would stay in that community for some period of time. He would make sure his teachings had been properly understood and that the community had forged a fervent commitment to their newly found faith before moving on to another community.

Before departing those communities, Paul would establish a leader from that community as their bishop. That bishop would then be responsible for protecting, growing and expanding the size of the community.

Therefore, the fact Gerontius was documented to be a disciple of one of the apostles, it must have been an apostle that traveled to the Baetica province and named Gerontius as its Bishop. There are other possibilities as to how Gerontius might have been named Bishop of Italica, but the one that would make the most sense is if he was named by an apostle that founded that community. The only apostle from early Church history that has been documented to have been in Hispania, and further to have been in the Baetica Province through oral tradition, is Paul.

We know that there is another oral tradition that exist of an Apostle having been in Hispania in the first century, and that was St. James the Elder. St. James was executed in Jerusalem in the year 40 AD. The tradition that he was in Hispania, which began much later in the IX Century, has him only visiting the northern, mostly unpopulated, areas of Hispania and not the south. The Catholic Encyclopedia has documented that this tradition is dubious given several historical inconsistencies and issues with it that makes it even harder to confirm than Paul's trip to Hispania. Nonetheless, I believe this tradition is so strong that we must respect it. This does not take away the possibility that St. James preached in the north of Hispania and Paul in the south.

Therefore, the historical documentation of Gerontius having been Bishop of Italica in the 90's AD, named Bishop because of his leadership of that community, and who was also a disciple of one of the Apostles, points to only Paul having been that Apostle.

There are other less intense oral traditions that Paul had been in Hispania. One such tradition is that he visited the cities of Salamanca and Merida, which could both be reached with relative ease from Italica following "La Via de la Plata." This was an important, protected, and heavily traveled trade-route of the Roman Empire during Apostolic times. It would have been about a ten-day walk to Merida, with plenty of places to stop, rest, eat, and sleep.

Therefore, although written documentation from inside Hispania of Paul having traveled there has never surfaced, there are several strong oral traditions that indicate that he was there. These oral traditions add to the overwhelming body of evidence that Paul did in fact make the trip.

So, there we have it! There is just too much written evidence from outside of Hispania as well as oral traditions from inside of Hispania that go back uninterrupted to Paul's time, that indicate he was actually there on a missionary trip. And we also have the oral traditions from the Eastern Orthodox Churches that are convinced Paul definitely travelled to Hispania.

How can we ignore all of these historical factors and traditions? As many historians will tell you, there have been many historical events and stories documented as fact with less documentation to support them. These all support the arguments and premise we are making in this book that Paul indeed made the trip.

There is, however, one important contrary position, that of Gelasius, Bishop of Rome, in the year 496 AD. Given how important this controversial issue is to the premise of this book, we dedicate the entire Chapter-6 in order to provide an in-depth analysis.

CHAPTER 6

HIGHLIGHTING ONE CONTRARY POSITION: GELASIUS-1, BISHOP OF ROME IN THE YEAR 496 AD

So far, in the previous chapters of this book, we have provided a number of very compelling and convincing historical elements that indicate Paul was able to complete his high-priority trip to Hispania. These include biblical writings, the direct testimony of Clement-I in the year 96 AD, the Muratorian Fragment from the second century, the apocryphal Acts of Peter from the second century, the six highly respected Doctors of the Church from the first four centuries of Church history, and the several additional oral traditions from within and outside Hispania that attest to Paul having made the trip.

When you combine this overwhelming documentation, you can easily see why the early Christian communities took it as a matter of fact that Paul travelled to Hispania.

This documentation, however strong as it might be, does not include any from the Churches inside Hispania. This point can easily be explained. That we cannot find additional definitive documentation from churches inside Hispania does not mean that it never existed, as some have argued. Keep in mind that early Christian books and writings were burnt and destroyed by the many Roman persecutions of Christians. This was followed by the 700 years of Muslim presence in Al Andalus, when they also destroyed Christian books and relics. And let's not forget that the subsequent Christian presence in Hispania after the fifth century was predominantly Visigoth Christian that had Germanic roots, and likely had little knowledge or tradition related to Paul.

The point we make here is that there is a tremendous amount of evidence that Paul travelled to Hispania. The fact no written evidence exists from churches inside Hispania cannot be used as a contrary argument since there are valid historical explanations as to why that's the case. And we also cannot ignore the very strong oral traditions from inside of Spain as well as from the Eastern Orthodox churches.

There is, however, a very important but controversial reference from the year 495 AD by Gelasius-I, Bishop of Rome. Keep in mind that the concept of a Pope did not yet exist until after the sixth century. It was Gelasius who began to aggressively promote that idea, espousing the argument that the primacy of the Church and its theological directions should come from the direct line of Peter, who had been the first Bishop of Rome and Vicar of Christ.

Fig. 27: Pope Gelasius; 492-496AD[80]

Gelasius was one of the most prolific writers and biblical historian of the early Church bishops. In the middle of one of his extensive and important encyclicals, which covered a number of issues, he included the following very simple reference about Paul not being able to complete his trip to Hispania[81]:

> "... There are times when one proclaims what will be done only to find later that it was not done for various reasons. Like the blessed Apostle [Paul], who promised going to Hispania in support of his evangelizing mission but did not go due to divine disposition. There is no need to think that the blessed Apostle was deceitful—no, God helps us—or contradicted himself because he promised to go to Hispania and later could not fulfill that promise impeded by higher causes. As far as his will, he said what he truly wanted to do; later he had to abandon this purpose due to dispositions from above, since he, as a man, although filled by the Spirit of God, could not know the secrets of divine disposition."

Many biblical historians have questioned why Gelasius would have written such a definitive reference disregarding Paul's trip. He was a distinguished Church historian, so he had to be aware of the strong tradition from the early Christian churches that Paul had been in Hispania. He makes this statement, contradicting the accepted tradition that Paul had been there, and yet never mentions the direct testimonial of Clement-I, nor the references from the Muratorian Fragment and the Acts of Peter, nor the writings of the other six distinguished Church Doctors. As a biblical historian, he must have at least known of the direct testimony provided by Clement and should have known of the other evidence supporting Paul's trip. He also must have been aware that Paul's visit to Hispania was a well-accepted tradition in Christian communities of the first 500 years. And yet, Gelasius disregarded all these facts by not even addressing them in his statement, and simply proclaimed that Paul did not make the trip.

Is it possible that Gelasius, known as an important Church historian of his time, not be aware of at least a couple of these important references to Paul having made the trip? As has been presented thus far in this book, there was significant historical evidence that indicated it was an accepted reality by many Christian communities during Gelasius time that Paul had travelled to Hispania. Had Gelasius made a positive comment in regard to Paul's trip, or no comment at all, perhaps history would have been written in a way to confirm that Paul made the trip.

That Gelasius would make such a definitive statement, contradicting what was accepted as a historical fact by earlier Christians, has made many historians question the wisdom, or perhaps more pointed, the motivation, for making such a statement. I, myself, have questioned it since Gelasius offered no proof or historical perspective to contradict the significant amount of evidence and tradition of Paul's trip to Hispania. He simply "proclaimed" that divine disposition did not allow Paul to go, and ignored making any reference to all of the evidence and tradition that pointed to the fact he made the trip.

Since Gelasius' statement has become one of the strongest arguments used by those that have opposed the premise that Paul visited

Hispania, I felt it was important to analyze his controversial statement. To do so, I discovered that it was vital to first understand the context of what was happening with Christianity at the time.

I began by going back to Gelasius' statement itself. We know he was fully aware that Paul had placed a very high priority on his missionary goal to evangelize the gentiles of Hispania. In fact, in his own statement, Gelasius mentions that Paul, "... *promised*..." going to Hispania in support of his evangelizing mission but did not go due to "divine disposition." The word "promised" confirms that Gelasius was aware of Paul's *very high priority* to travel to Hispania.

Gelasius also had to be aware that in Paul's second letter to Timothy, covered in Chapter-2, Paul clearly states that he "...finished the race...". This statement by Paul to his most trusted disciple, Timothy, clearly implies he successfully accomplished his "promise" of going to Hispania. This conclusion is especially supported when placed in the context of everything Paul had as a high priority. Many biblical historians today agree with this interpretation of Paul "finishing the race," and Gelasius, as a distinguished historian, must have at least been aware of the implication of this reference from Paul.

As a biblical historian, therefore, Gelasius should have been aware of all the elements mentioned in the previous chapters supporting the missionary trip to Hispania by Paul. And he also had to be aware of the strong oral tradition that existed in Christian communities, especially in the Eastern Christian communities founded by Paul.

So why would Gelasius contradict these sources without offering any further documentation himself to support his statement disregarding Paul's trip?

My assessment, and answer to this question, provides a very intriguing and perhaps controversial analysis of Gelasius' intentions. We can only speculate of what his intentions could have been, but there are some very definitive factors that could have influenced his decision to remove any importance of Paul having been in Hispania.

We begin by looking into the fact that Gelasius was involved in several difficult conflicts with the Eastern Churches of the time. He had inherited from his predecessor, Bishop Felix of Rome, the struggles with the Eastern Roman Emperor Anastasius, and with Euphemius, the Christian Patriarch of Constantinople. These struggles centered on controversial positions that had been taken by Anastasius and Euphemius.

Gelasius then complicated matters even more by insisting on several controversial edicts he developed that were not acceptable to Eastern Churches. This included a highly controversial edict for the Eastern Churches: that the primacy, or highest religious authority, over the entire Christian Church (East and West), needed to come from the line of Peter's succession. He then explained that the bishops of Rome, including him, were in fact the line of Peter's succession.

To support his argument, Gelasius used the statement from Jesus himself. In Mathew 16:18, Jesus established Peter as the head of the Church, *"...You are Peter and upon this rock I will build my church..."*. Since Peter had been the first Bishop of Rome, and established as the head of the Church by Jesus, then all subsequent Bishops of Rome would also take on the role of the head of the Church.

The Eastern Churches were not in agreement from the moment Gelasius pushed this premise as a Church doctrine. Why? Because for the early Eastern Churches, Paul was considered equally important to Peter. Paul was the founder of the majority of the Eastern church communities. He was also the first to recognize that Christianity was not a separate sect of Judaism but a completely new religion that evolved from Judaism. Paul even instituted a number of practices to force Jews who converted to Christianity to slowly stop practicing the "Laws of Moses" [82].

Gelasius was thus the first Bishop of Rome to begin aggressively promoting the premise that the Bishop of Rome had a direct line of succession from the Apostle Peter. This premise, presented around the year 495 AD, would later be used by future Bishops of Rome to continue to assert the supremacy of the Roman Bishop over all Christians. It would eventually be converted into a doctrine by the Catholic Church, leading to one of the main conflicts that led to the full separation of the Eastern Orthodox Churches from the Roman Catholic Church in the year 1054.

To understand the additional difficulties rooted in this specific conflict, we must go back in history to put into proper context how the Christian Churches had organized themselves in early Christianity. By the fifth century, Christendom was divided into five regions known as Christian Patriarchates, with the highest-ranking bishop in each established as its Patriarch. These five regions were: Rome, Constantinople, Jerusalem, Alexandria and Antioch. Each region's patriarch would be responsible for overseeing the Church in that region.[83] In the case of Rome, it was the religious center for the Western Churches, which included Hispania.

Right from the beginning there were a number of critical issues that separated the Patriarchate of Rome from the other four Patriarchate. One of the most important differences was the language and culture of the Roman church, with Latin as the language and Roman traditions as their culture. This was a major contrast with all four of the Eastern Churches, which had Greek as their language and Byzantine traditions as their culture. These differences in language and culture created major issues in political positioning when deciding on major edicts and doctrines. We can add to these conflicts the perspective held by the Eastern Churches that saw both Peter and Paul as "equals" in establishing Christianity, with Peter not being any greater than Paul. The Roman Patriarch and the Church communities that fell under him, however, always favored Peter over Paul.

It is important to note here that the official Church doctrine establishing the primacy of the Pope was not established until the year 1073 by Pope Gregory VII, several centuries after Gelasius first presented this premise[84]. Following Gelasius' encyclical on the subject, however, the term "Pope" (el Papa, which means "father") began to actually be used in the VI century in western Christian churches to refer to the Bishop of Rome as well as to other highly distinguished bishops[85]. Thus, beginning back with Gelasius, this became a major issue that raised the intensity of the difficult conflicts that existed between the Roman and Eastern churches. It eventually led to the famous "Schism" that broke apart Christianity in the year 1054 AD into the Roman Catholic Church and the Eastern Orthodox Churches.

We can only speculate, but with these very difficult conflicts beginning at the end of the fifth century with the Eastern Churches, one could argue that Gelasius' focus and energy would not have been placed in matters such as Paul's visit to Hispania. However, if this situation was examined with a critical eye, the argument could also be made that this was precisely the reason why Gelasius would want to disregard the possibility that Paul founded the churches in Hispania. The conclusion could easily be reached that given the importance the Eastern Churches had placed on Paul, it was not in Gelasius' best interest to give Paul an important position or presence in regard to the churches in Hispania[86]. Since Paul never wrote an epistle to the Hispaniards, Gelasius could have used that premise to declare Paul never made the trip.

It's important to recognize that Hispania had to have been a vitally important region for the early Church, and in particular for the Roman Patriarch. Therefore, given the controversy that was brewing between the importance of Peter versus Paul, it would have been in Gelasius' best interest to find a way to deflate and divert all links of Paul having been in Hispania. One could speculate that the last thing Gelasius needed was to also have had Paul established as the founder of the Churches in Hispania. That could have led the churches in Hispania to also take aggressive positions against the premise that the Bishop of Rome, as Peter's successor, should have primacy over all Christianity.

By discounting Paul's missionary trip to Hispania, whether done with an ulterior motive or whether Gelasius truly believed Paul never made the trip, the fact is that his declaration provided perhaps the strongest argument used by those opposed to Paul having made the trip. Gelasius could then focus on the much larger and growing conflict with the Eastern Churches, thereby avoiding another conflict in the West.

These arguments could explain why Gelasius contradicted all the other very credible sources of information. By making such a simple statement against Paul's trip, without offering any proof to counter such a strong set of evidence in favor of Paul's trip, he laid the foundation for arguments against Paul's importance to Hispania.

Of course, history has shown that perhaps Gelasius was right with his premise that the line of bishops that descended from Peter should have the primacy of the Church. You can certainly argue that the Roman Catholic Church has played an important role at the global level in a number of different ways. Although the Church and some of its Popes have had scandals and controversies, the historical fact that we can now appreciate is that the Catholic Church appears to have had the hand of the Holy Spirit to help it grow and strengthen as a global institution. The response to any criticism of Popes, of course, has been that these were imperfect men, and that their actions will eventually be judged by God above.

The critical analysis conducted herein is not meant to deemphasize or discard the statement by Gelasius, but to provide proper context on his statement. Readers can then draw their own conclusions. The simple assertion being made here is that given Gelasius reputation as a biblical historian, he should have been aware that the early tradition of the Church included Paul's visit to Hispania. Had he not written his negative assertion of the trip, there would probably be little doubt today that Paul had indeed completed his "promise" of traveling to Hispania to convert its gentile population. In fact, had he gone the other way and confirmed the trip, as the overwhelming traditions during his time indicated, Paul's trip would have been a certainty today.

CHAPTER 7

THE FAMOUS COUNCIL OF ELVIRA IN GRANADA, YEAR 302-304AD: DOES IT SUPPORT THE PROBABILITY THAT PAUL PLANTED THE CHRISTIAN SEEDS FOR THESE COMMUNITIES?

Fig. 28: Left—Today's Albaicin neighborhood of Granada, where the Roman town of Iliberis was located around the year 300, on top of the mountain range Elvira. Ancient documents indicate the Council of Elvira took place in the Roman Forum there; however, no ruins have survived. **Right**—Immediately across the river valley from the Albaicin is where the fabulous Alhambra Palace was built around the year 1238

The earliest recorded Christian Council in Church archives, where policies and rules for Christians to live by were written down and documented, took place in the Roman town of Iliberis, today's Granada in Spain. It took place most likely between the years 302-304[87]. This council included a large number of Christian communities from across Hispania coming together to establish rules for Christians to follow in their daily lives. The town was situated within the mountain range known as Elvira in what today is the Albaicin neighborhood of Granada.

The exact date of the Council is a matter of some disagreement, but there is no doubt it took place prior to any other known Christian council where canons, which are Church rules and norms, were confirmed in writing. There were 81 such canons confirmed in this Council. In addition to the fact original documents still exist, archived in the Vatican, references to this gathering of Christian leaders were recorded in later councils and in other important early Church documents. It became known as the Council of Elvira. Present were 19 bishops plus a large group of presbyters representing 37 Christian communities from Hispania, most of which were from the Baetica Province in the southern Roman region of Hispania[88].

What gives this Council a very high level of significance is that it was the first known gathering of a large early Christian region whose leaders recognized that they needed to establish rules and norms for their community of Christians to follow. The fact that such a large gathering, with such an important goal, took place in Hispania and not in Rome, Greece, or Asia Minor, confirms the advanced level of understanding of Christianity that existed in Hispania.

Christian leaders there understood that in addition to their Christian beliefs, standards for how Christians needed to conduct their lives had to be established across all Christian communities in Hispania. A number of very important canons came out of this Council, including Canon 33, the first mandate in Church history that established the celibacy of bishops and presbyters, with a penalty of excommunication.

It should be noted here that there were two earlier important councils in Antioch in the years 264 and 269 AD that brought together various church communities from the Eastern churches. These councils, however, were held to discuss the issue of whether Jesus Christ and God were of the same substance. There were no written canons or norms for Christians to follow coming out of those councils.

I would like to therefore draw special attention here to the fact that all 37 Christian communities and the 19 bishops who signed and authorized the resulting canons were all from the region of Hispania.

What conclusion can we draw from this fact?

Given that there were no bishops from any other region of Christendom, it is a critical point to make here that those present felt they had the authority to establish norms based on the tenet of their Christian beliefs. Those bishops must have felt empowered by an earlier Christian authority that had been given to them, in order for them to believe they did not have to check with Rome, or any other Church, to establish their 81 canons.

We know that there were fairly close relationships between the Church in north Africa and Hispania, and some historians have theorized that perhaps Christianity in Hispania evolved from north Africa. But we need to pay very close attention to this very specific fact being presented here: there was no authority figure from Africa, from Rome, or from anywhere else, at the Council of Elvira, other than the bishops of Hispania. And yet, those bishops established and authorized some of the most important rules for Christians to live by that have been recorded in Church history, many of which are still in effect today.

In all my research surrounding the Council of Elvira, I have yet to find any mention of this particular insight. Those bishops, acting independently from any other early church region, came up with those very detailed and very strict set of Christian norms. They didn't check with any other Christian region to have their canons approved. They understood that they didn't need to check with any other "Christian Authority." They did it on their own.

Think about that for a moment. The canons established at Elvira imposed very strict rules and a very rigorous set of disciplines for Christians to lead their lives. There was no reconciliation with the Church for certain sins including adultery, incest and idolatry, among others. Those sins resulted in being excommunicated from the Church forever. For lesser sins, the person was excluded from Holy Communion for a very extended period of time. Members of the Clergy were expected to follow a celibate and holy life, and those falling away from these rules were quickly excommunicated. There were a number of very strict rules dealing with matrimony, confessions and communion. And they established all these Christian rules and norms under their own authority.

Perhaps an indication of how important the Council of Elvira was is the fact that many of its canons were adopted and included in later councils, including the Council of Nicaea only 23 years later. Considered the most important council in the history of the Church, the Council of Nicaea is from where the Nicene Creed comes from, which laid the foundation for what Christians believe in.

Some biblical historians have wondered, including myself, how the Christian community of Hispania could have grown independently of the rest of Christianity to have reached such an advance level of understanding of this new Christian religion. And more importantly, that they understood they had the authority bestowed on them to develop such important sets of rules, norms and canons.

Here is where the premise being presented in this book comes in, that it had to be an individual with a very high Christian authority who established Christianity in Hispania. The evidence I have researched and presented in this book indicates that it was the Apostle Paul.

It's hard to get around this very specific point. For the Christian bishops of Hispania who participated in the Council of Elvira to have proclaimed that these very strict rules had to be followed by all Christians, they absolutely must have understood that the authority to do so had been bestowed on them. We can only speculate, but reason tells us that this authority must have been given to them by someone very close to Jesus Christ himself.

That authority figure must have also felt a certain level of independence from the Church in Jerusalem, allowing the Church in Hispania to understand they had independent authority bestowed on them from Jesus Christ himself. The only Apostle who fits that description is Paul of Tarsus.

It's actually a very important fact to highlight that a number of important Christian leaders, all from Hispania, participated in the Council of Elvira. In that regard, perhaps one of the most important Christian leaders was the subsequent emergence of Osio, Bishop of Cordoba (Hosius in Latin). Osio was named Bishop of Cordoba in the year 295, and as will be discussed later in this chapter, he became an extremely important figure in early Christianity.[89] In the case of the Council of Elvira, many biblical historians have concluded that Osio played a critical role in bringing together the 37 Christian communities of Hispania present at the council.

Osio is listed in second place in the list of Bishops that signed the canons that came out of the council, with Felix, Bishop of Acci (today's Guadix in the Andalucía community) as the first signature. Acci represented the oldest established Christian community in Hispania, established around the year 67 AD, so it is understandable why Bishop Felix, also one of the oldest bishops in the council, was the first signatory to the document. That Osio was listed second would indicate he had a high-level within the group of Bishops present, and for sure, as the Bishop of Cordoba, Capital of the Baetica Province, he must have been considered one of the Council's leaders.

Fig. 29: This image of Bishop Osio was used as the cover for the book: *Osio de Cordoba, 2013*. It depicts Osio towards the end of his influential life

Osio must have been a highly capable statesman to be able to navigate the many difficulties Christians had to face with Roman authorities. As the capital city of the Baetica Province, Cordoba had become one of the most important centers of trade and commerce for the Roman Empire by the second Century AD. As discussed in Chapter-2, the Baetica Province had become a Roman "Senatorial Province," so Cordoba as its capital was also the center for Roman government authorities and an important military outpost.

In spite of the various periods of Roman persecutions during the first 250 years of Christianity, the community of Christians in the Baetica Province was able to establish itself and grow. This is obvious by the large number of communities from this province that participated in the Council of Elvira. Many biblical historians have concluded that in order to have this large presence of Christians by the end of the third century, a very charismatic and energetic Christian authority figure must have started it all in the first century. The distinguished biblical historian, Fr. Manuel Sotomayor from the theological faculty of Granada, makes this specific point in his highly acclaimed seven volume work on the Catholic Church of Spain.[90]

Someone with a high degree of Christian authority had to have gone through Hispania and the Baetica province, established communities, and named leaders in charge of those communities before departing. Reason tells us that only an individual with the credibility of a charismatic Christian leader, one whom the community understood had the direct authority from Jesus or the Apostles, could have had such an impact as to permanently plant the seeds and ingrain this new religion on the people of Hispania. Through this individual, who could connect gentiles and Jews, could such an advance Christian community have evolved.

So, the Council of Elvira is in itself, testimony in favor of the argument that someone like the Apostle Paul would have founded Christianity in Hispania.

The fact no one else has surfaced as the confirmed founder of the Church in Spain or the Church in the Baetica province actually allows for the arguments that it was Paul. For sure, the subsequent emergence of a number of Christian Church leaders, including Osio, that earned such a high level of credibility, would indicate that the roots of their Christian instruction had to have come very early from someone with a very high level of authority for Christianity. Let's therefore continue to explore some of the more important details concerning the timing as well as the historical context surrounding the Council of Elvira.

Biblical historians all agree that the Council took place sometime between the year 300 and 314 AD, with the years 302-304 being the most commonly cited time frame by recent historians, and one that I agree with[91]. This period took place before the brutal persecution launched against Christians by Emperor Diocletian towards the end of the year 303 and beginning of 304, which lasted until 312 AD.

It's important to place this period into proper historical context and note that the Roman Empire was being ruled at the time as a Tetrarchy. This governing structure called for one emperor for each of four imperial regions (see map Fig. 30). Diocletian, who launched

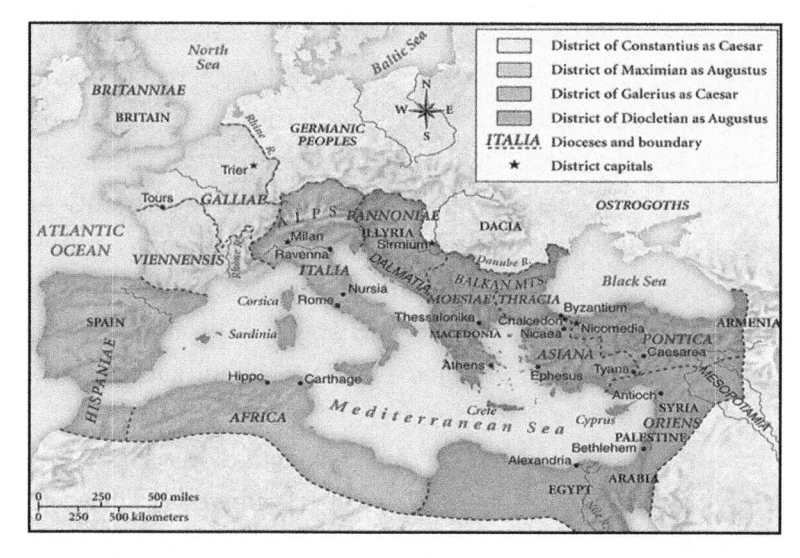

Fig. 30: This map represents the Roman Tetrarchy that existed around the year, 300 AD[92]

the Christian persecution of 303/304 AD, ruled over a region which included large parts of Asia Minor, Palestine and Arabia. Early in 304 AD, he was able to convince the other three Roman Emperors that Christianity was an afront to the Roman Empire and that they should persecute Christians in their regions. Two of the other three emperors, however, Constantius and Maximian, who ruled over the two western tetrarchies, were never interested themselves in pushing this persecution, although they allowed their governors some flexibility in doing so.

The reason the exact year of the Council of Elvira is not known is that the original documents refer to the month it was held, but not the year. However, by knowing the dates of the persecution launched by Diocletian, it would be illogical that the Council would have been held during the Diocletian persecution, between years 304 and 312.

Historians are therefore forced to estimate the actual year of the gathering based on the Council taking place no later than the beginning of 304 AD. They also estimate it did not take place earlier than

300 AD based on dates some of the bishops present were named to their positions.

From a historical perspective, it is important to note that there were other critical developments soon after 304 AD involving the northern and western Roman Empire that impacted early Christendom and the evolution of Christianity in Hispania.

The northern Roman Tetrarch, which included Britain and France, was inherited by Constantine in the year 306 AD after the death of his father Constantius, who had never been aggressive at persecuting Christians. In the following years, a number of battles evolved between the northern and western tetrarch to consolidate those regions and establish sole rule of the Western Roman Empire under Constantine.

History has documented that Constantine was converted to Christianity during the final battle to consolidate his region of the empire. Constantine went into that final decisive battle in the year 312, against then Emperor Maxentius, the son of ex-Emperor Maximian, who ruled the western tetrarchy district that included Hispania and Italy. In spite of being significantly outnumbered, Constantine defeated him, and in the retreat Maxentius drowned trying to escape across Italy's Tiber River[93].

It's been documented that before that critical battle began, Constantine saw a Cross in the sky with the following words next to it: *"IN THIS SIGN YOU SHALL CONQUER.*[94]*"* The sign Constantine saw was the Christian Cross.

After his victory, Constantine began the process of removing any persecution of Christianity in the region he governed. That was an important turn of events that launched the consolidation and future growth of the Christianity[95].

Now that he had become the Western Roman Emperor, Constantine joined the Eastern Roman Emperor, Licinius, in signing the "Edict of Milan" in the year 313 AD. This edict ended the persecution of Christians and provided all citizens the freedom to worship regardless of religion. Keep in mind that Hispania was now fully under the

Fig. 31: Painting depicting Constantine vision of a Cross and the message: "In this sign (Cross) you shall conquer." By Giulio Romano—1520: *The Battle of the Milvian Bridge*

juridiction of Constantine, so a number of projects were launched to build Christian churches there.

Conflicts continued, however, between the Western and Eastern Roman Empire and in the year 324, Constantine was able to consolidate complete control of the Empire (the details of this consolidation are extensive, so we leave it up to readers to explore this historical fact separately). He then established his center of government in the city of Byzantium, and changed its name to Constantinople, today's Istanbul.

Of special interest on how Christianity had evolved in the Baetica Province is the fact that even after Emperor Diocletian in 304 AD encouraged the other Emperors and the governors of the Roman provinces to persecute Christians, the persecution of Christians in Cordoba apparently never took place. Many historians believe it was likely that at that time Osio had positioned himself as a master statesman who was able to manage the protection of his entrusted Christian flock. We know that there were some persecutions in Hispania at the beginning of the IV century since some local governors used Emperor Diocletian's persecution to position themselves politically, but hardly any documented in Cordoba.

So, although Maximian, who had the tetrarchy that included Hispania, was not pressing for such persecutions, there were some local governors who still went ahead to make examples of a few Christians leaders to show those communities the need to renounce their Christian faith. The martyrdom of St. Vincent, patron saint of Valencia and Zaragoza, is a good example of this. In this case, the Governor of Hispania's Province of Carthaginensis in the year 304 AD had St. Vincent tortured and executed in order to set an example[96]. In spite of the most horrendous and barbaric tortures, St. Vincent would not denounce his faith, and his martyrdom became well-known throughout early Christianity.

Thus, an important argument being presented here is that all indications point to Bishop Osio being able to deal with this very complex set of dynamics to protect his Christian community. And in fact, his name and level of importance in early Christianity grew in importance over the following 40 years.

And here is where an important connection is made between the enormous influence of the Christian community of Hispania and of Osio, who emerged as one of the most prominent Christian leaders in early Christianity, with the way he connected to Emperor Constantine.

Shortly after Constantine authorized Christianity as a legal religion in the year 312[97], Bishop Osio was summoned by Emperor Constantine to become one of his spiritual advisors. There is little information available as to why Constantine made this request. This is an interesting dynamic that requires more research since Constantine and his father had previously ruled the northwestern empire regions of Brittanie, France and Gaul before taking over Hispania in 312 AD.

There is no evidence, nor does it make sense, that either Constantine or his father would have had close Christian relationships with the southwestern region of the empire prior to 312 AD. This southwestern region included Hispania and Italia, which were part of the tetrarchy of Maximian. And yet, in spite of this major geographic disconnect, shortly after Constantine wins the war against Maximian and takes over this tetrarchy, his conversion to Christianity begins and, in the process, calls for Osio to become his spiritual advisor.

We therefore ask the question: Why did Constantine ask for Osio to become his spiritual advisor? We can only answer that by using "deductive reasoning" to reach the logical conclusion that Osio must have been one of the highest respected Christian leaders in Christendom by the year 312. He must have been considered even more important than the Bishop of Rome since by this time Constantine's tetrarchy included all of Italy. Constantine must have somehow known, or become aware, of Osio's reputation, as well as that of the well-established and advanced Christian communities of Hispania.

We then ask another question: What major historical event would have established that Christianity in Hispania was so well advanced as to have given Constantine the knowledge and confidence to ask for Osio of Cordoba in the year 312? We can only answer that question with another deduction: that the Council of Elvira had become well-known throughout the Christian communities of the time, including Brittanie and Hispania.

A lot of the dynamics surrounding these circumstances come full-circle when we consider that Constantine was also responsible for assembling the Council of Nicaea in the year 325 after he consolidated the Empire in 324. The Council of Nicaea is still considered the most important Council in the history of Christianity, even to this day. It was the first "Ecclesiastical (Ecumenical) Council" of the Christian Church[98]. Not only was it attended by 318 bishops from all over the Christian world[99], it also established a number of critical beliefs and canons of the Church. In fact, the main beliefs of Christianity were captured in what we know today as the Nicene Creed.

A critically important point for this book is that at the same time Constantine convened the Council of Nicaea he also asked Bishop

Osio to preside over the Council. That Constantine did not ask the Bishop of Rome, nor the Bishop of Constantinople, nor any other Bishop, to preside over the Council of Nicaea, would indicate that he must have attributed to Bishop Osio a very advanced level of understanding of Christian precepts. In doing so, he was also attributing indirectly a very high level of understanding to the Christian churches of Hispania. In fact, given that the Council of Elvira took place around 22 years prior to the Council of Nicaea, and that Bishop Osio had a principal role in convening that Council, a deduction we could make is that Osio himself could have made the recommendation to Constantine that a universal Council should be held.

Although there's ambiguity concerning the interactions between bishops during the proceedings of the Council of Nicaea, it's interesting to note that there's not an extensive amount of historical context or information on those proceedings. One would think that the Church would have published the details of those proceedings, but the number of publications on this subject is very limited.

We do know, however, that there were deep divisions that occurred with some of the eastern churches concerning the teachings of Arius of Alexandria, who claimed that Jesus was not "Divine," but a being created by God. This position directly contradicted the belief of the majority of the Council's participant that Jesus was indeed one with God and from the same substance, from which the doctrine of the Holy Trinity emerged.

Perhaps to avoid surfacing this controversy even more, the Catholic Church has not expanded historically on the proceedings of the Council of Nicaea. This would explain why so little is known about the fact that a Bishop from Hispania led the Council, and that he could have steered the discussion in favor of the doctrine of the Holy Trinity. It is also interesting to note that the Catholic Encyclopedia,[100] as well as some biblical historians, have also concluded that it was Osio who likely suggested convening all the Bishops of Christendom for a universal council of the Church. Either way, whether or not Bishop Osio was responsible for the eventual convening of the Council of Nicaea, what remains well documented in Church documents is that he was the Bishop that presided over the Council[101].

The discussion on the Council of Nicaea shines a light on the importance of the Council of Elvira and its participants since it preceded Nicaea. Some of the bishops who were at Elvira were also in Nicaea,[102] including Osio, thereby providing a representation of bishops from Hispania at the Council of Nicaea.

With regard to Elvira, the bishops present in that council not only discussed the rules for how Christians should run their lives, but they also discussed the principle tenets of the Christian religion in order to properly address those rules. The fact is well documented that attributed to the Council of Elvira were 81 canons, or rules for Christians to live by. Therefore, by the time the Council of Nicaea took place, the canons documented in Elvira must have already become well known in Christian communities outside of Hispania.

The rules and canons coming out of the Council of Elvira have provided an important window into the religious life of Christians in Hispania and also in most of Christendom in the years that followed. They dealt with a lot of every day elements including the strict life of the clergy as well as frequenting Mass, the relations between Christians, Jews, and pagans, the need for fasting on special celebrations, rules related to marriage, baptism, etc.[103]

Perhaps it would be important here to actually detail two of the more important canons dealing with the life of the clergy, Canon 18 and Canon 33:

> *Canon 18: Bishops, presbyters and deacons, if—once placed in the ministry—they are discovered to be sexual offenders, shall not receive communion, not even at the end, because of the scandal and heinousness of the crime.*

Cannon 33 represents the oldest known ecclesiastical ordinance in Church archives concerning the celibacy of the clergy

Canon 33: Bishops, presbyters, and deacons, and all other clerics having a position in the ministry, are ordered to abstain completely from their wives and not have children. Whoever, in fact, does this shall be expelled from the dignity of the clerical state.

These very strict rules were established by a Council in Hispania ... not in Rome, nor Alexandria, nor in Antioch, nor in Jerusalem. They were established in the Council of Elvira in Hispania. Under what authority did these bishops feel empowered to make such strict rules, many of which were later adopted by all of Christianity?

These bishops understood that they had the authority to do so. We can therefore see how critically important the Council of Elvira was in the evolution of Christianity.

We end this chapter with the clear conclusion that the Council of Elvira was an important predecessor to the Council of Nicaea, and that the canons coming out of it played a critical role in how Christians were to conduct their lives. Also playing a critical role was Bishop Osio of Cordoba, who presided over the Council of Nicaea.

These two facts alone allow us to conclude that the concepts, or precepts, of what it meant to be a Christian had to have advanced in Hispania to a unique level within Christendom. For sure, we can conclude that at the very least, the Baetica region in particular, had reached among the most advanced levels of early Christianity.

The above conclusions, therefore, lead us to again confirm the premise of how critically important the ecclesiastical leaders of Hispania were, and how the tenets of Christianity evolved to such an advanced level there. These laid the foundations to the establishment of a very devout Christian stronghold in the Iberian Peninsula that not even the subsequent Muslim invasion, several centuries later, could completely eradicate. We know that because after the Muslim invasion of 711 AD, the slow but non-stop process of recovering their Christian lands by the Christians who were able to survive in the northern region of Asturias, happened because of their deep devotion to Christianity. It took over 700 years, but the deep faith of the Christian Kings and the Christian people of Hispania, overcame and re-conquered their Christian lands from the Muslims.

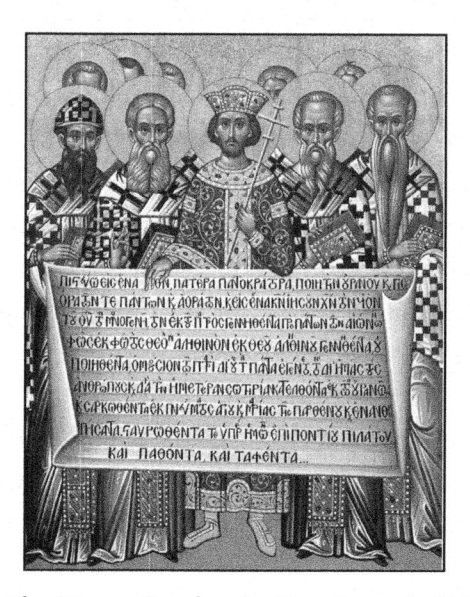

Fig. 32: The Nicene Creed at the First Council of Nicaea[104]

We continue these arguments and research findings of how important Hispania/Spain has been to the evolution of Christianity in the following chapter of this book. In regard to the Council of Elvira, there is no doubt that the advance level of Christian beliefs developed in Hispania had the "imprint" of coming from someone like one of the apostles, who I propose was Paul. I have presented these arguments to acknowledge and leave no doubt of the enormous influence Hispania had very early on with the evolution of Christianity.

CHAPTER 8

IN THE TRUE MISSIONARY SPIRIT OF PAUL, HISPANIA/SPAIN'S ULTIMATE MISSION: THE RECOVERY, PROTECTION, AND EXPANSION OF CHRISTIANITY

I'm going to start this chapter by getting right to the point. There has been no other region in the world that has had such an immense impact in the expansion of Christianity as the two countries that today make up what was previously the region of Hispania in Roman times: Spain and Portugal. Spain in particular, led the largest evangelization of the Americas, which today represents the biggest block of Christians in the world. You could actually argue that what Spain really expanded in the Americas was Catholicism, the biggest denomination of Christianity.

Together with that expansion has come some controversy as it has been accused of abusing the life of many indigenous people in the Americas. That is what some Christian Protestant groups pushed early in the Protestant Reformation in what some have referred to as an attempt to defame the Catholic Church. Known as the "Black Legend," these attacks have been mostly unsubstantiated by numerous historical accounts published over the past 100 years.[105]

So, why did Spain have such an impact in the expansion of Christianity? When you do a deep analysis, you realize it started way before the evangelization of the Americas and that you have to go back to early Apostolic times.

As discussed in the previous chapter, the Council of Elvira provides a strong testament to the fact Christianity grew to a very advance level very early in the evolution of the religion. Many biblical historians believe that for the religion to have evolved as it did, it must have been because of a very intense missionary effort by a very charismatic apostle, or perhaps by a group of disciples of one of the Apostles. It would be illogical to think that such an extensive number of Christian communities that had advanced to such a high level of understanding of Christianity would have evolved any other way. It certainly would not have been from a few Christian merchants or roman legionnaires settling in the peninsula like some historians have claimed.

As mentioned in the previous chapter, the Council of Elvira demonstrated that the 19 bishops present felt they did not need the authority of any other Christian leader to establish its 81 rules and canons. Their direct authority must have been established two centuries before by a missionary effort by someone with an exceptional talent for conversions, but more importantly, with the authority to bestow the bishops he named with the same authority. Otherwise, the bishops in the Council would have felt the need to receive approval from a higher source before requiring the very strict rules that came out of Elvira.

The premise presented in this book is that Paul was responsible for that missionary effort. The fact is that regardless of who was responsible, it instilled a burning commitment on the early Christians of Hispania to this new religion, and the subsequent kingdoms and Christian kings.

As I continued to connect all the research pieces, I realized Hispania had a very special Christian history that needed to be told, not just because of its early Christian history, but perhaps even more important, because of what followed.

I therefore decided that a portion of this book needed to be dedicated to bringing to light how this deep devotion to Christianity evolved, especially since there were a number of mostly unknown historical factors that I felt needed to be highlighted. Through my research, I began to "connect" a number of points that led to some interesting insights of how Christianity evolved throughout the peninsula. These insights were so clear, that they led me to conclude that no other country in the world played such an important role in the evolution, protection and eventual expansion of the religion during its first 18 centuries.

What therefore began as a personal quest ten years before the publishing of this book to determine if the Apostle Paul had been in Hispania on a missionary trip, evolved into the conclusion that he indeed made it. But in addition, it also led me to realize that biblical historians have not really given Spain its proper place in history when it comes to the evolution of Christianity.

Through my research and discussion with priests and biblical historians, I realized that there was very little knowledge of how important the early Christian communities of Hispania had been to the evolution of the religion. The previous discussion in Chapter-7 on the Council of Elvira is an example of how little information has been published on the importance of Hispania on the history of Christianity. When I discuss this point, even with many members of the clergy in Spain as well as in the U.S., almost all of them are surprised. Most of them had no idea that Hispania/Spain played one of the most important roles in establishing the tenets of the religion during the first three centuries of Christianity.

So, what are the proof-points to reach this conclusion. We can provide a quick summary here and later in this chapter get into a much more detailed discussion on each of the critical historical elements.

As covered in Chapter-7, we know of Hispania's early influence because of the extensive documentation that came out of the Council of Elvira, 302/304 AD, which took place in what is today the City of Granada, Spain. Again, this was the first Council in Church history to have documented the rules and canons that Christians needed to follow in their daily lives. These rules were later picked up by other Councils.

We also know that Bishop Osio of Cordoba, who was one of the leaders in the Council of Elvira, became one of the most important leaders in Christianity during the early part of the IV Century. How do we know? Because Emperor Constantine chose him to preside over the Council of Nicaea in 325 AD. This is considered the most important Council in the history of the Church. The fact Constantine chose a Bishop from Hispania, and not the Bishop of Rome, or of Constantinople, or any other bishop, tells us Osio must have been seen as a "Leader among Leaders" of the early Church. This confirms that Christianity in his region of Cordoba in Hispania, had to have reached the most advanced levels of its time.

As I continued my research, I realized that the difficulties the Roman Empire was having in the V Century, allowed the Visigoth Christians to begin moving into Hispania, and by the end of the VII Century they had settled over the entire peninsula. The Visigoths were then taken by surprise by the sudden and rapid Muslim invasion of Hispania in 711 AD. This Muslim army swiftly crossed from Africa with an overwhelmingly large and experienced army, and with the help of internal Visigoth enemies, had taken over almost the entire peninsula by the year 722 AD. Only a small group of Christians in the northern, mountainous peaks, in the region of Asturias, remained unconquered and defiant.

For the ensuing seven centuries, the Christians kingdoms of what had been in Hispania showed tremendous tenacity in their efforts to recover their Christian lands, and never lost their Christian faith. They showed that same true spirit and "grit" that Paul had shown during his thirty years of missionary efforts.

Then in 1492, after Granada, which was the last Muslim kingdom, fell to the Crown of Castile, the most important expansion in the history of Christianity began. Castile comprised what was previously the largest kingdom of Hispania. Its Queen, Isabel-I, advocated for the expansion of missionary trips to new lands discovered by Columbus in the Americas by signing an edict ordering every ship going to the "New World" to take two missionary priests with them. These missionary priests were instructed to remain in order to convert to Christianity the native "Indians" of these new lands. History tells us that these missionaries became so immersed in the lives of the natives in their missions, that they gave their lives in many cases to protect the natives of these new lands.

With these major historical facts in front of me, I was going through a process where insights way beyond the original scope of my research kept coming up.

So, you might ask, why is the subject matter of this chapter so important? The answer is that during those 15 centuries that followed the Council of Elvira, the people of Hispania actually grew in faith. They were also instrumental in large part in first keeping the religion from being exterminated by the Muslims, and later, for keeping the flame of Christianity alive. And then, they led to the most impressive expansion of the religion.

Through my research, it became evident that a "national consciousness" rooted in the Christian faith evolved in the people of Hispania during the first seven centuries of Christianity. A sort of deep Christian "Heritage" had evolved, rooted in the belief and devotion to Jesus Christ, but also, and perhaps even deeper, to Mary his Mother.

In fact, the people of Hispania developed over those centuries a very special and deep devotion for the Virgin Mary. There are countless stories and references to the reverence shown by the early Kings and people of Hispania to Mary as the Mother of God. From the Visigoth Christians in the VI Century, to King Pelayo of Asturia in 722 AD, through the Spanish Christian Kings of the Middle Ages, through King Fernando III, the Saint, in 1248 AD, through Queen Isabel and King Fernando in 1492, and even until today with King Felipe VI—through all these centuries—a tremendous and fervent devotion to the Virgin Mary has been intensely held by the people of Hispania/Spain. There is no doubt that today in the XXI century, even when attendance in the Holy Mass in Spain has been declining, the devotion to the Virgin Mary, Mother of God, is still fervent throughout the country.

It was this immense dedication to their Christian faith and devotion to the Virgin Mary that spearheaded the process of reconquering the lands lost to the Muslim invaders in the VIII Century. And, as soon as they were done reconquering their lost lands at the end of the XV century, they embarked on the largest expansion of Christianity in the history of the Church. This resulted in the Christianization of most of the Americas and the Philippines.

The Christianization of the Americas was not an accident. As mentioned in the previous page, it was spearheaded by Queen Isabel after she and her Husband, King Fernando-II of Aragon, conquered the last remaining Muslim Kingdom of Granada in 1492.

Isabel sponsored Columbus' trip that resulted later that year in the discovery of America. A very devout Catholic who was also devoted to the Immaculate Conception of the Virgin Mary, Queen Isabel signed an edict in 1496 mandating that every ship going to the Americas had to take two missionary priests to stay and evangelize the native people of these new lands.[106]

Many explorers and families followed, with the stated purpose to remain, evangelize and populate these newly discovered lands. In doing so, they were bringing Christianity to stay, and in particular Catholicism, with the Pope as their religious leader.

It's important to take a moment to go back and note that the recovery of Hispania from the Al Andalus Emirate, and later Caliphate, by the various Hispanic Christian kings, took seven centuries (711AD-1492AD). They did it without any direct military support from anyone else, including the Catholic Popes. It was the dedication to Christianity by the people of Hispania and their kings that led to the full recovery of their lost lands and the merger of several kingdoms into what we know today as Spain.

The importance of the Popes should not be diminished, however, since they provided a certain level of authority to the Spanish Kings' efforts. It's also important to be clear that the Kings of Hispania were very loyal to the Pope. They clearly understood and believed in the concept that the head of the Church descended directly from the Apostle Peter, the first Bishop of Rome, as instructed by Jesus Christ himself. In fact, history shows that the Spanish Christian kings became the main protectors of the Popes because of their belief that the direct line back to Jesus needed to be respected and protected.

Of especial mention is that Pope Alexander VI in 1494, gave Fernando and Isabel the title of "Catholic Monarchs" to highlight the importance of their support of Christianity, the Church, and the veneration of the Virgin Mary. These two monarchs were also responsible for the unification of the kingdoms of Aragon and Castile, which established the majority of the region we know today as Spain.

Fig. 33: Catholic Monarchs: King Fernando and Queen Isabel

Perhaps we should also mention one more reference by a Pope to Spain's veneration of the Virgin Mary as the Mother of God. In

2003, Pope John Paul II travelled to Spain to lead the celebration of the canonization of five new Spanish saints. When he finished all the events and was now giving his final remarks before embarking back to Rome, the Pope made the following farewell in recognition of Spain's devotion to the Virgin Mary: "My great love for you, Farewell Spain! Farewell Land of Mary!"[107]

Had it therefore not been for this powerful devotion to their Christian Faith and the Virgin Mary, the intense effort of the Hispanic kings to recover the territories invaded by the Muslims in the eighth century, Christianity as we know today may not have survived. One could argue that there were political or materialistic reasons for the Spanish Kings' efforts to take back those territories, but it was their documented devotion to Christianity, and in particular to the Virgin Mary, that drove their intense efforts.

The establishment and growth of Christianity in the Americas can be attributed in large part to the same Christian focus. Just look at the hundreds of missions that were established by the Spanish missionary priests, or to the names the Spaniards gave to the cities they founded: Los Angeles, Santa Fe, San Francisco, San Diego, Sacramento, etc., etc., etc.

In this discussion we should not ignore Spain's neighbor to the west, Portugal, responsible for the Christianization of Brazil. Hispania, with its strong Christian roots, covered the two countries of Spain and Portugal, and although they emerged as separate countries, they both continued to grow a strong religious fervor in favor of Christianity and the Virgin Mary.

This book would therefore not provide a complete picture on the crucial role Hispania played in the growth of Christianity if we didn't expand on the above-mentioned efforts by the Spanish kings and its people to recover their Christian lands. It's therefore important to provide further details and the historical context that led to these efforts.

We begin with a discussion on how the Visigoth Christians ended up moving into Hispania and summarize the actions of some of their kings, followed by a discussion on the Islamic invasion of Hispania and the importance this period of history had on the Iberia peninsula.

A. Growth of Christianity in Hispania by the Visigoths in the VI and VII Century AD

If we follow the expansion of Christianity in Hispania through the first six centuries, documented in large part with continued Christian councils after the Council of Elvira, we see that by the beginning of the VI Century the Visigoth Christians had moved south from northern Europe to settle in Hispania.

The Visigoths were filling the void left by the fall of the Roman Empire and established their kingdom with Christianity as the official religion. At the same time, they allowed Jewish communities to exist as long as they followed heavy restrictions on the public practice of their religion[108].

Since Christianity had already spread throughout Hispania after Constantine allowed Christianity to grow in the Roman Empire, the Visigoths were accepted by the local populations. There was some level of reluctance at first since they brought the Arian denomination of Christianity where most of the Christians of Hispania were Nicaean Christians.

As previously explained in the Arian vs. Nicene discussion during the Council of Nicaea, the Arians believed that Jesus Christ was not of the same substance as God but was a separate being created by God as his son, where the Nicene Christians believed Jesus was of the same substance. This difference apparently did not have a major effect on the population and frictions were soon dissipated.

Fig. 34: This map shows that by the year 700 AD, the Visigoths had taken over all of Hispania, and established Toletum as their capital[109]

As shown in Fig.34, over the next two centuries, Christianity would become the religion of all of Hispania. Historical records have documented that Visigoth King Liuvigild in 568 AD established Toletum (Toledo) as their capital and kept the previous name of many of the Roman provinces the same[110].

An important king that followed was King Recared, son of King Liuvigild, who was responsible for consolidating into the Visigoth kingdom the remaining small portion to the south held by the Byzantine Empire, previously the Roman Empire.

As mentioned in the previous page, the Visigoth's were mostly "Arian" Christians. A well-documented event in the evolution of Visigoth Christianity is when in the year 587 AD, Recared converted to Nicene (Catholic) Christianity. He changed his belief and supported the Catholic tenet that God is the Father, and Jesus was the Son, but of the same substance as the Father.

Fig. 35: Famous Painting by Antonio Muñoz Degrain, 1887, showing the conversion of King Recared to Nicene Christianity in 587 AD

It was in the Council of Nicaea where the belief was established that God the Father, Jesus the Son, and the Holy Spirit were the same, while Arian Christians believed that Jesus was the Son of God, but not of the same substance in every aspect.

The large, almost full-wall painting shown in Fig. 35, depicts the moment King Recared converted to Nicene Christianity in 587 AD, and with this act, the entire Visigoth kingdom was also officially moved from Arian to Nicene Christianity. This is a very famous painting that marks an important moment in the continued evolution of Christianity in Spain, and currently hangs in public display in one of the most important rooms of Spain's Senate building.

B. Islamic Invasion of Hispania

The Islamic invasion of Hispania, which began in the year 711 AD, happened very quickly. Islamic leaders took advantage of deep divisions within the Visigoth's kingdom and the fragmented loyalties that existed with different Visigoth family factions.

Although the Visigoth kings were aware of the rapid expansion of Islam after it was founded by Mohamad, they were taken by surprise at the bold move by the Umayyad Caliphs to cross from Africa into Hispania in 711 AD. The Muslims were helped by the hatred that had developed against the Visigoths by Jewish leaders living in Hispania.

These Jewish leaders provided important strategic information to the invading Muslims, and that allowed them to move quickly against the Visigoths, creating chaos in their defenses. The Visigoth King, Roderic (Rodrigo), and his army, never had a chance to properly prepare for battle against the large invading Muslim army.

In the chaotic battle of Guadalete in the year 712 between the Visigoths and the Muslim invaders, Roderic and most of his senior leadership were killed, sending the kingdom into total disarray.

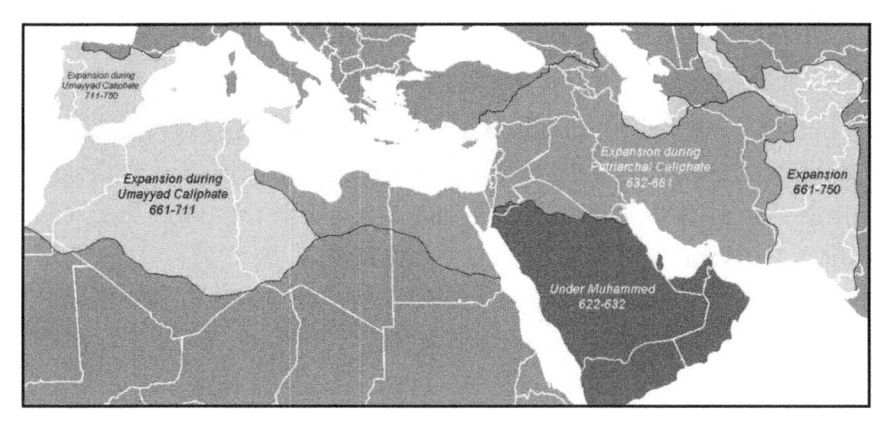

Fig. 36: Shows rapid expansion of Islam throughout the Middle East and Africa. Shows expansion into Hispania by the Umayyad Dynasty[111]

In a very short time, by the year 718 AD, most of Hispania, with the exception of the small northern region known as Asturias, had fallen to the Muslims. As shown in Fig. 36, in less than 100 years, Islam had expanded from its origins in 622 AD in the Arabian Peninsula, to most of the Middle East, North Africa and most of Hispania.

It's important to note that the animosity that existed against the Christian Visigoths by the Jewish leaders was so intense, that they felt conspiring to help the Muslim Umayyads would be better for them and their families. With their help, the Muslim Umayyad generals were able to take control of Hispania.

We should emphasize that the Umayyad Dynasty was the first great Muslim dynasty that grew largely out of the Merchant family of the Quraysh tribe in Mecca[112]. They created a fast-moving army that could easily exert its military power over the mostly nomadic tribes that made up the initial Muslims communities in the Arabian Desert.

When this invading army of soldiers, made up of mostly desert tribesmen, reached Hispania, they were so impressed with the green fields, flowing waters, and fertile lands that they fell in love with this new land they had conquered. They named this new land Al-Andalus, which some historians have roughly referred the name in Arabic "To become green at the end of summer."[113]

With their rapid expansion, however, and with other internal and external conflicts, the Umayyads suffered a number of political and military defeats around the same time they had conquered Hispania. In the year 750, the end of the dynasty came to a disastrous defeat in the Battle of the Great Zab River in a region that is today Iraq.[114]

After that battle, all the members of the dynasty were hunted down and executed, with one exception, Abd al-Rahman, who managed to escape to Hispania and position himself as the Muslim Emir ruler in Al-Andalus.

Fig. 37: Abd al-Rahman I, Emir of Kurtuba in 756 AD[115]

Once Abd al-Rahman took control of Al Andalus, with Kurtuba (the Islamic name for Cordoba) as the capital, he continued the Umayyad Dynasty creating the Emirate of Kurtuba in the year 756.[116]

A significant historical fact is that in recognition for the support the Muslim armies received from the Jewish leaders, Abd al-Rahman I allowed them the freedom to practice their religion, but with some restrictions in deference to Islam.

The region of Al-Andalus continued to strengthen in its Islamic presence and in the year 929 AD it was designated a Caliphate under Abd-ar-Rahman-III.

Most historians have documented that by the end of the first millennium, Cordoba, the capital of Al Andalus had become the largest city in Europe. It was one of the most advanced cities in the sciences, medicine, philosophy, mathematics, and the arts. In the appendix to this book, I have provided a summary of the importance of Al Andalus to the Jewish and Islamic religions, and in that summary, I highlight the advanced civilization they created.

C. The Recovery (Re-conquest) of Christian Hispania from the Muslims

After the initial invasion by the Islamic forces in 711 AD, a small Christian enclave was able to establish itself in a region high in the mountain peaks of the region known as Asturias. Because of its difficult topographical location in the mountains, the Muslim forces did not bother to try to completely root them out at first. That small Christian population in Asturias, however, did not give up and continued to revolt by launching small skirmishes around the boundaries they had created between their territory and the surrounding Al Andalus territory.

What began as small skirmishes would eventually become seven centuries of a continued effort by the Christian people and kings of Hispania to recover their previously Christian lands. This highlights the fact that the Hispanic Christian kings never gave up on taking back those territories that were once Christian lands. Volumes of books have been written about this recovery, or re-conquest as is mostly referred to in history books, so I don't pretend to provide here a full historical narrative. It is important, however, that we provide a summary of the more important elements of this recovery so we can place it in the proper historical context.

Critical in the re-conquest of Hispania was that the Muslims were never able to expel the small Christian forces in the northern region of Asturias due to two important factors. The first was the logistical challenges created by this extreme mountainous region. The second and most important, was the bravery of the Christian people of Asturias and the leadership of Pelayo, who became their king. Historical accounts of Pelayo vary greatly, but the majority of accounts confirm the story of how he became King over the small remnants of Visigoth Christian lands in northern Spain after the Muslim had decimated the Visigoth kingdom in the invasion of 711 AD.

Historians universally credit Pelayo with beginning the recovery of Hispania from the Muslims in the name of Christianity. For this reason, we will provide here an extended account of how important he is to the History of Spain today. Maps will also be provided to show the progression over the centuries of the recovery of the previously Christian territories invaded by the Muslims.

The account of Pelayo's rise begins with the defeat of the Visigoth King Roderick (Rodrigo in Spanish) in the Battle of Guadalete in 712 shortly after the Muslims invaders crossed into Hispania. The defeat came in this major battle, which took place in the southern region of Hispania. As previously mentioned, Roderick and the Visigoths had been betrayed by his political opponents as well as the Jewish leaders in Hispania who provided the Muslims with strategic information on the Visigoth forces. With the quick victory, the invading Muslim army was able to advance north over the following seven years and take Toletum, the capital of the Visigoth kingdom. They continued north during the next couple years and successfully occupied most of Hispania. For the mountainous region of Asturias, the Muslims were only able to establish an administrative/military outpost close to the region under the direction of the Muslim General Al Kamah.

Fig. 38: Statue of Pelayo found at the foot of the Mountain of Covadonga

Pelayo was a younger cousin of King Roderick, and as an accomplished warrior, became a member of the King's personal guard. During the aftermath of the chaotic battle scene of the Battle of Guadalete, in which Roderick lost his life, Pelayo was able to escape. He was able to regroup with a small force and continued north, first to the capital Toletum to warn its residents and few remaining members of the king's court, and then to the mountainous region of Asturias.

In the year 718, in a gathering of fellow Visigoth Christians of Asturias, Pelayo convinced them that they needed to fight back against the invaders. His passionate appeal quickly led to Pelayo becoming the leader of what was becoming a growing number of Visigoth Christians escaping from Muslim lands. He made it clear to them that the war they were waging was for the survival of their Christian heritage. He was then able to field an army of approximately 1,000 well-trained and experienced armed men and led them in a number of skirmishes over the next four years. These skirmishes were meant to weaken the Muslim military outpost and to convince the Christians in the region to resist. General Al Kamah, in charge of the military outpost, seeing that the skirmishes continued, asked for reinforcement from Toletum to end the resistance and completely take over Asturias once and for all.

Historical accounts have documented what followed next, although there are several variations. Most historians agree with the version that in the year 721, an Islamic army reported to be of 300,000 (perhaps somewhat exaggerated), crossed into France to try to take over that large region known as Aquitaine, of which Toulouse was its most important city. After an initial victory by the Muslims in which they took Toulouse, the Duke of Aquitaine was able to gather a large army himself, and in a surprise attack, overwhelmed the Muslims, handing them a major defeat. The retreating Muslim force was able to regroup in northern Hispania and a force reported to be of 60,000 soldiers (some reports say 40,000, others 30,000) was organized under General Al Kamah to attack the small Asturian forces and end the insurrection of Pelayo.

When Pelayo was informed that an overwhelming force of Muslim soldiers had been organized to invade Asturias, he and his men fortressed themselves in and around a cave in the Mountain of Covadonga. The cave and surrounding cliffs offered a major strategic advantage to the greatly outnumbered Christians. To prepare for the battle, they piled thousands of large stones that could be launched down the mountain, and also prepared thousands of arrows that could be slung from on high. While they waited for the enemy to finally reach the mountain, Pelayo went back inside the Cave of Covadonga, where he had placed a statue of Our Lady, the Virgin Mary.

When the Muslim invaders arrived and prepared for battle, the Muslim general asked for Pelayo's surrender just before the battle was to begin. Pelayo would not surrender and began to pray with his troops before the start of the battle. He asked the Virgin Mary for special protection in the coming battle since they all expected to die in the name of Christianity. At that moment, Pelayo looked to the sky and saw a Cross coming down, and the voice of the Virgin Mary called out that he and his men would be victorious.

Once the battle began, Pelayo's men fought ferociously from the top of the Mountain. Legend, combined with historical accounts from Christians, but especially from Arab historians, recount what followed. The Muslims began the attack with hundreds of archers sending arrows at the Christian forces behind the stone cliffs. As this first attack unfolded, and Muslim soldiers began climbing the mountain, something astonishing happened. The arrows being flung by the archers turned back and started killing many Muslim soldiers. Seeing that the arrows were not reaching them, a group of Pelayo's man started openly throwing stones and shooting arrows at the Muslim soldiers. Another group of Pelayo's experienced fighters began to fiercely attack the Muslim soldiers that were coming up the mountain and were viciously defeating them. In the heat of battle, the second Muslim official in command fell dead and disorder ensued. General Al Kamah then gave the order to retreat.

At that moment a huge storm hit the mountain sending very heavy rains and lightning into the entire area. The heavy rains caused major boulders to become loose and mudslides began to come down on the Muslim soldiers, many of whom were buried by the mud and others slipped all the way down to the nearby Deva River where they drowned. After suffering enormous casualties, Al Kamah ordered a complete retreat at which point Pelayo's troop attacked in an even more ferocious way. The Muslim General Al Kamah was killed in the battle and the retreating Muslim forces returned back to Toletum completely defeated.

Nobody knows for sure since historical accounts vary, but most accounts list Pelayo's forces only lost 100 men or less, while the Muslims lost anywhere between 6,000 to over 10,000, plus many thousands injured. After word of this victory spread, thousands of Christians still living in the occupied Muslim regions fled to Asturias, and the added forces fueled the efforts to continue the recovery of Hispania in the name of Christianity.

In my research, I found a captivating account by the Catholic News Agency on why Pelayo chose the Cave of Covadonga to fight the Muslims. This account has been mostly verified by other historians. Here is the Catholic News Agency version unedited:[117]

> *"It is said that Pelayo found this cave, years before the battle, one day when he was chasing a criminal. When Pelayo chased the man into this cave he was stopped by an old hermit monk who had hidden the fugitive in the cave. The hermit monk said,*
>
> *'If thou wilt pardon this culprit, and give him time to repent his sins, thou too wilt someday find a haven in this holy cave, and through thee there will be born a new and powerful empire, which shall make thy name a glory to thy people for all time.'*[118]
>
> *Pelayo granted the hermit's request. He later dedicated the region, including the cave, and his army to the Blessed Virgin*

Mary, Mother of God. He would also pray openly that he and his small army would be able to defeat their powerful enemy and that the Christian faith would be preserved. Not long after this incident, when Al Kamah and his army approached, Pelayo remembered this cave and it was there that he took his men to wait for the enemy, determined to either conquer or perish in the fight."

The inspiring story of Pelayo's prayer and battles have been well documented by historians. His story is similar to that of the subsequent Christian kings in that the Virgin Mary was evoked in prayer prior to the many battles they had to fight against Muslim forces.

With the slow but successful efforts to recover their lost lands in the name of Christianity, there were small Christian principalities created. Over the years these became Christian kingdoms. We see in Fig. 39 that by the year 900 AD small kingdoms were already being formed under the various feudal kings in the region[119].

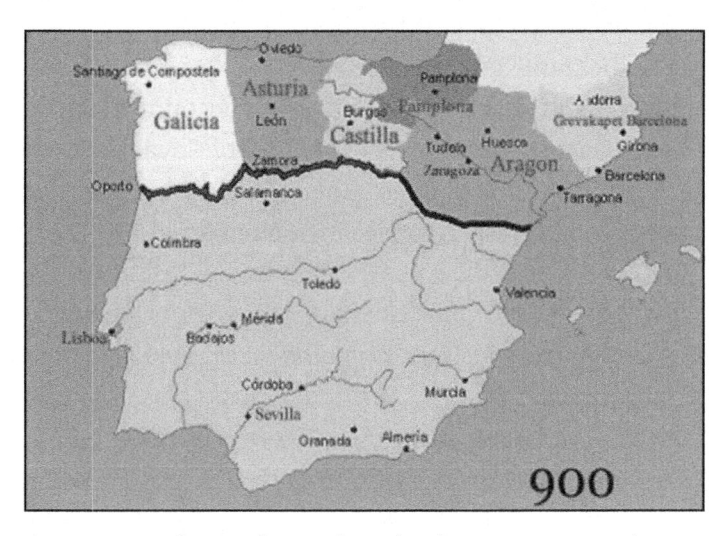

Fig. 39: Map of Spanish Kingdoms by the year 900[120]. Light Gray area represents Muslim Al Andalus.

These smaller kingdoms were created with Christian traditions, but they were constantly aware of the presence of the Muslim military governors just to the south. To stay alert on the potential attacks by Muslims, a line of castles was built along their southern borders to ensure that not only they could slow down or stop any advancing Muslim force, but to also provide advance warning to their kings.

During the 200 years that followed, there was increasing turmoil and upheavals within the Muslim world.

The battles between Muslim groups outside and inside Al Andalus created instability and allowed the Christian kings to continue to recover their lost lands. As a result, Christian forces were able to take advantage of that turmoil, especially since many of the residents in those lands had been Christians subjugated to the Muslim rules imposed on them. As shown in Fig. 40, by the year 1100 the Christian kingdoms had recovered considerable territory.

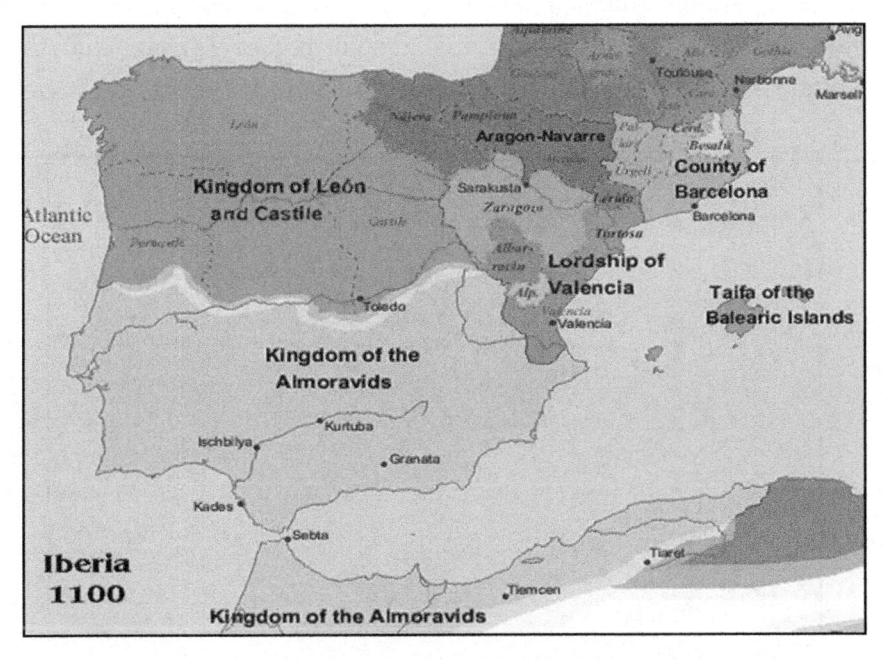

Fig. 40: Kingdoms of the Iberia Peninsula in the year 1100 AD[121]

By this time the kingdoms of Leon, Asturias, Galicia, and Castile merged, as well as Aragon and Navarra. Valencia had also established itself as a separate lordship. The Umayyad Dynasty that had ruled the Caliphate of Cordoba and Al Andalus for three centuries was defeated in the year 1062 and replaced by the new Muslim Dynasty of the Almoravids. The Almoravids Dynasty was an imperial Berber dynasty that was created in the year 1040 from nomadic Berber tribes that moved throughout the Sahara and the northwestern territories of Africa.

The Almoravids established their capital in Morocco but given their constant expansion through northwestern Africa, it was only a matter of time before they would attack and expand into Al-Andalus.

The turmoil and internal conflicts between Muslim ruling groups continued, and in the year 1147 the Almoravids were overthrown by the Almohades in Morocco, and subsequently, by 1172, took over the Almoravid's territory in Al Andalus. With the upheaval and chaos between Muslim ruling groups, the Christians continued to gain territory. By the year 1212 the Christian kingdoms had now expanded to the bottom half of the peninsula and were consolidating strength and power.

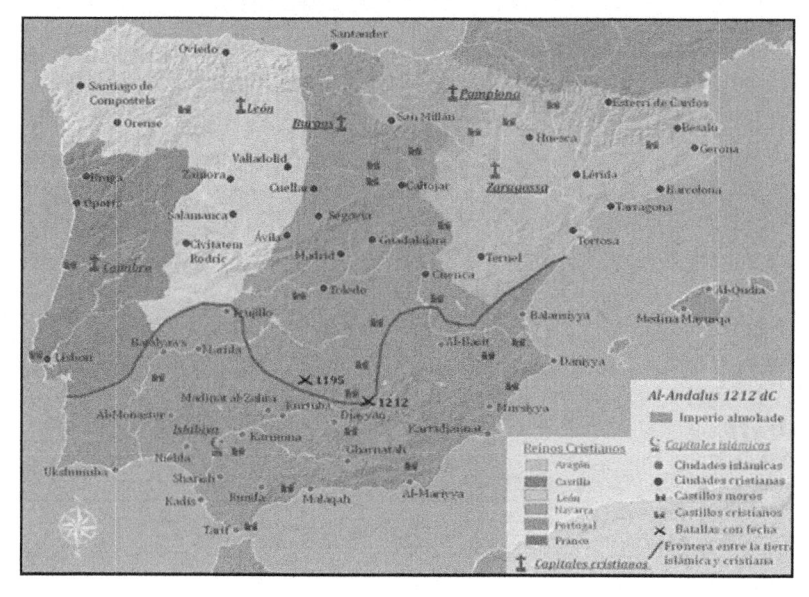

Fig. 41: As shown by the dark boundary line, by 1212, the Caliphate of Al-Andalus had been reduced with the expansion of the Spanish kingdoms and the emergence of Portugal[122]

In fact, while the Muslim kingdoms were being fractured, the Spanish Kingdoms were actually going through a process of consolidation. During this period in the Middle Ages, the Christian kings realized they needed to work together as a joint force against the Muslim rulers of Al-Andalus. Therefore, there was a significant level of cooperation that evolved between these kingdoms. There were always political issues, and in some cases even skirmishes between them in order to control their feudal kingdoms, but there was also cooperation against the greater danger posed by the Muslims.

The kingdom of Portugal was also created during this Muslim turmoil, and it allied itself with the existing Christian kingdoms against the Muslims, who continued to face instability and internal battles from other Muslim dynasties.

Then, one of the most important expansion of the Hispanic Christian kings followed with King Fernando III.

Fig. 42: King Fernando III

Fernando first secured the permanent union of the Kingdoms of Castile and Leon, which had been split a century before. He was the son of a previously arranged marriage between Berenguela of Castile and Alfonso of Leon, both of whom eventually ascended to the throne of their kingdoms.[123] With the combined forces of a unified kingdom and the continued alliance with the kingdom of Aragon, he was able to take back the Muslim stronghold of Seville, and right after that, Cordoba, the capital of the Caliphate. By 1248, he had recovered most of the remaining region of the Christian Visigoth lands and left only the small kingdom of Granada under Muslim control after an agreement was signed with the Muslim king.

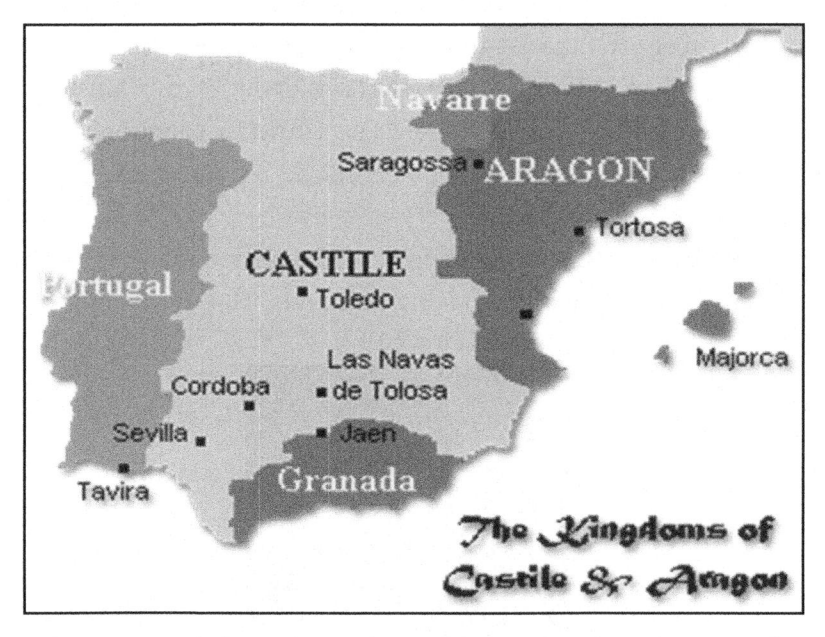

Fig. 43: Map of Christian Kingdoms of Hispania and Muslim Granada by the year 1270

As shown in Fig. 43: By the year 1270, after the unification of the kingdoms of Castile and Leon, as well as Aragon and Navarra, and the recovery of lands by King Fernando III, the only remaining Muslim Kingdom was Granada.

King Fernando was canonized in 1671 by Pope Clement-X for the documented victories and miraculous events coming from his fervent belief in Christianity and the Virgin Mary. His campaigns were always in the name of Christianity, but he also had a deep devotion to the Virgin Mary. Historians have written extensively about Fernando being a master at using both military strategies as well as diplomatic initiatives. They credit these strengths for the great success he was able to garner in the reconquest of so much territory. By the time he was done with the recovery of those territories, he had managed to isolate the remaining kingdom of Granada. During the following 240 years, the kings of Granada entered into treaties with the Christian kings and maintained a more stable relationship between kingdoms, but their attitude of peaceful coexistence would eventually end.

It was because of the political skills of the Muslim kings of Granada that they were able maintain relationships with the Spanish kings for those 240 years. Eventually, with the wedding between Queen Isabel, of the kingdom of Castile, and King Fernando, of the kingdom of Aragon, the unification of both kingdoms led to what is known today as Spain. Together they directed the surrender of the king of Granada in January 1492.

Of special interest is the way the Kingdom of Granada was brought down, a process that took ten years. Rather than a continuous war, King Fernando and Queen Isabel executed the battle as a series of seasonal military campaigns, starting each year in the early spring and ending in the beginning of winter. As they neared the many towns on the various paths to Granada, they would first ask for the town's surrender, which most did, thereby avoiding more bloodshed with its residents. If the town denied, they would take limited military action by surrounding the town and limiting the amount of goods getting in until the town surrendered. This process also placed significant pressure on the Muslim kings since there was little they could do to prevent the advance of the Spanish forces.

This process also took advantage of the internal political conflicts that were taking place with the Muslim dynasty between the Sultan Abu-I-Hasan, his son Abu Abd-Alah Mohamed XII (Boabdil) and the Sultan's brother Mohamed XIII (el Zagal). The Spanish strategy was to slowly isolate the walled city of Granada, which included the

Muslim King's Alhambra palace. The Alhambra was the home of the Muslim Emir of Granada, better known as King Boabdil. Through this strategy, the Christian kings were slowly surrounding Granada and cutting off all routes for supplies and reinforcements.

Knowing that time was on their side, King Fernando and Queen Isabel actually went to the frontlines once their army got close to the walled city. In late 1490, they established a field command center that they named Santa Fe (Holy Faith), at 13 kilometers (approx. 8 miles) from the City of Granada. Finally, on January 2, 1492, King Boabdil surrendered the Emirate of Granada and the Alhambra palace to the Castilian forces.

Fig. 44: Painting by Carlos Luis de Ribera y Fieve, *Conquest of Granada*, 1890, Burgos

In the famous painting depicted by Fig. 44, we have Isabel and Fernando praying with the palace entourage from their encampment at Santa Fe for the surrender of Granada. They were hoping to avoid bloodshed by slowly cutting food and supplies and forcing Boabdil to surrender.

After a 10-year campaign, on January 1492, the Muslim kingdom of Granada ended. Isabel and Fernando quickly converted it to Christianity. In Fig. 45, we can see the very famous painting of

Boabdil surrendering Granada to Isabel and Fernando. The painting, *The Capitulation of Granada*, is by Francisco Pradilla Ortiz, 1882, and is on display in the Spain Senate Building.

Fig. 45: *The Capitulation of Granada* by Francisco Pradilla Ortiz, 1882

There is an interesting historical anecdote on the reconquest of Granada. A legend exists that as the Royal Muslim party moved south toward exile, led by King Boabdil, they reached a hill, stopped and looked back to see the amazing Alhambra and the city of Granada. Boabdil then started to cry. His mother looked at him, and sternly admonished him by saying, "You are weeping like a woman for what you could not defend as a man."

For their part and without knowing it at the time, Isabel and Fernando began the most important expansion in the history of Christianity after the fall of Granada. Isabel in particular, approved the trip of Christopher Columbus to the "Indies," which as we know today, turned out to be the Americas. There are numerous documented records that show that rather than finding any riches, Isabel's goal was much more the Christianization of the people Columbus would meet.

In fact, she passed an edict making it mandatory that on every government sponsored ship to America two missionary priests needed to go and stay for the purpose of evangizing the local populations.[124]

In 1494, for their commitment to Christianity, Queen Isabel and King Fernando were bestowed the title of the "Catholic Monarchs" by Pope Alexander VI. The Spanish kings that followed also continued to support the efforts to evangilize the Americas. As a result, hundreds of missions were established all throughout the Americas and the Caribbean. These efforts also extended to the Philipines and even to other asian/pacific territories.

There are over 1.2 billion Catholics in the world today, with about 60% of them in the areas colonized by the combined efforts of Spain and Portugal, both of whom have their origins back to Hispania.

Christianity as we know today, and in particular Catholism, may never have survived if not for the dedication, passion, and fervor to Christianity by the people of Hispania, beginning in apostolic times, continuing through the middle ages and into the XIX century. In that sense, it seems that "History" has not really given Spain the level of importance that it deserves, which is an important premise of this book.

There were a number of negative initiatives against Catholicism and Spain that evolved in the 1500's and continued for several centuries. One of those being the misguided "Black Legend" against Spain and Catholicism, which exaggerated facts about acts of cruelty by Spain, for the purppse of blaspheming Spain as well as Catholicism. Numerous studies in the last centuries have shown those Black-legend stories used statistics that have been disavowed and renounced as not factual.[125]

Nontheless, the research and conclusions being presented herein have laid the foundation to support the fact that at the very least, Hispania/Spain had an immense level of importance in the evolution and expansion of Christianity, perhaps being as important as Rome when we consider the first 1500 years.

We can easily justify this last statement by recognizing the following. First, we have the fact that the tenets and beliefs of Christianity grew independently in Hispania to one of the most advanced in Christendom by the year 300. That growth and consolidation continued with the Visigoth Christian kingdoms, and by the year 700 the entire Iberian Peninsula had become a Christian stronghold. Followed by protecting and recovering the religion through the Middle Ages from probable extinction by the Muslims. And eventually with the best intention of converting new souls to the religion when it evangelized a major portion of the Americas.

When it comes to the Americas, testimony of this is that the biggest protectors of the newly discovered indigineous population were actually the Catholic missionary priests that followed Comlumbus.

In Chapter-10, we'll summarize all of the conclusions presented herein.

CHAPTER 9

ESTABLISHING THE STEPS OF THE APOSTLE PAUL IN HISPANIA

Given the extensive documentation provided in this book on Paul's missionary trip to Hispania, there are really only two conclusions we can reach:

a) that there is a very strong likelihood Paul went to Hispania, although a definitive statement should not be made since he never wrote an epistle to the Hispaniards, which is the position of many biblical historian; or,

b) that a **definitive statement should be made with the conclusion that Paul did in fact conduct a missionary trip to Hispania.** This is the position recent historians are reaching and one that I agree with, adding new arguments based on research I have uncovered.

Therefore, I add my name in a strong way to those that have recently reached the same conclusion, doing it using a scientific methodology resulting from my research. I am therefore strongly advancing the conclusion that Paul definitely made the trip. I am doing so by following the research analysis process that focuses on deductive arguments to reach a conclusion. This process follows the concepts behind the "Theory of Conclusion."[126] This theory stipulates the following three premises:

a) conclusions are statements which are accepted on the basis of unusually strong evidence;
b) conclusions are to remain accepted unless and until unusually strong evidence to the contrary arises;
c) conclusions are subject to future rejection, when and if the evidence against them becomes strong enough.

In this case, when we combine the totality of evidence presented that strongly point to Paul having conducted a trip to Hispania, the arguments in favor that he made the trip are much stronger than the single contrary statement from Pope Gelasius that he did not make the trip. The same is true for others who reference his statement and use a feeble discussion as to why he did not make the trip. Until somebody comes up with a definitive argument that proves Paul did not make the trip to Hispania, I am proposing the conclusion that he did, and back it up with the evidence presented herein and summarized in the following pages of this chapter.

As a researcher, I therefore conclude with a very high level of confidence that Paul conducted a missionary trip to Hispania. To summarize, I base the conclusion on all the evidence that has been presented in this book:

- Paul had established a very high priority for his missionary trip to Hispania, as he states in his letter to the Romans around 58 AD,

when he explains that he will stop in Rome only as a staging area for his planned trip to Hispania (Rom 15).
- Paul saw his specific mission as that of preaching and converting the pagan gentile, a mission given to him by Jesus Christ directly through Divine Revelation. I provided several New Testament passages confirming this point, where Paul's letters and Luke's Acts of the Apostles make it clear that Paul's main mission was to preach and convert the pagan gentiles.
- Hispania, especially the Baetica province, had one of the highest population densities in the Roman Empire, virtually all gentiles, and Paul was surely aware of that fact, making it a very important goal for him to go there and preach the Word of Christ. Unfortunately, when Paul tried to deliver to the Christians in Jerusalem the funds he had collected in Macedonia, around 59 AD, the Jewish leaders in Jerusalem became aware he was there. They conspired to trap him, and when Paul entered the Temple, they accused him of violating Temple laws and arrested him. They then turned him over to the Roman authorities accusing him of sedition (conspiring) against Rome. As a result, he was incarcerated and spent the next two years in a Roman jail in Caesarea, Judea, waiting for his trial.
- Paul then claimed his Roman citizenship and asked to be tried in Rome. He was then moved to Rome where he spent two more years in house-arrest while waiting for his Jewish accusers from Jerusalem to show up and confirm the accusation in a Roman court. Those Jewish accusers never showed up for fear they themselves could have been thrown in Jail. Roman law required that after two years, if the accusers did not show up, he would be set free.
- Then, the positive tone in which Luke ends Acts of the Apostle clearly implies Paul was freed from his two years in house-arrest in Rome, which would have been around 64 AD. He was either set completely free, or sent into a controlled exile situation,

which would certainly have been to Hispania. Based on information presented in earlier chapters, I have concluded he was set free. It also becomes clear he was set free when you consider that there are two years missing of his whereabouts after 64 AD. It is not until his second letter to Timothy, written around 66/67 AD, that there is an indication he was again back in a Roman jail. Those missing two years would indicate he was traveling since he always wrote his letters to a community after he had traveled there and not in the middle of his travels.

- That Luke makes no mention of what happened to Paul during those two years, especially after providing so many intricate details in Acts of the Apostles, has led some biblical historians to theorize that he (Luke) must have had plans to continue Paul's story in a separate book. That theory provides an explanation as to why Luke would have ended Acts so abruptly since he must have considered what followed Paul's freedom was so important that he felt a separate book was needed. That theory also leads to the speculation that Paul must have had great success in Hispania. Either way, with Luke ending Acts using such a positive tone, the only logical conclusion you can reach is that Paul would have been set free.

- Continuing with the conclusion Paul was set free, it is also logical to conclude that during the two-years of house-arrest in Rome he would have surely been making plans to travel to Hispania. Knowing his stubborn character as well as his talent for convincing new converts, and considering he was able to freely receive visitors, Paul would not have given up on his high-priority trip to Hispania. That stubborn character would have led him to recruit a few Roman followers to help him plan the trip. There is a strong oral tradition in Ecija that Paul recruited one of his disciples by the name of Hieroteo to go with him to Hispania. Hieroteo was a merchant from the city of Astigi, today's Ecija in southern Spain, who happened to be in the city of Pafos, Cyprus, when he heard

Paul preaching, and was converted to Christianity. With or without Hieroteo, since he was now so close to Hispania, it is completely illogical to think he would not have tried by any means to travel there. He certainly would not have gone back to Jerusalem or to any of the other regions where he had founded churches. So, once in Hispania, even with limited access, Paul would have been able to conduct missionary activities.

- As explained in Chapter-2, Section-F, in Paul's second letter to Timothy, Paul stated that he had "finished the race" (2Tim 4: 6-8). This is a strong indication Paul travelled to Hispania during those missing two years since that was one of his highest priorities. Timothy had to have known that preaching in Hispania was one of Paul's highest priority, so Paul's testimony that he had "finished the race," can only be interpreted that he was telling Timothy he had accomplished all his goals. Unfortunately, Paul was never able to write a letter to the Hispaniards after he left because he was executed soon after he returned to Rome.

- It is almost certain Paul would have entered Hispania through Tarraco, the military provincial capital of the Tarraconensis Province, the preferred entry port of ships coming from Rome. Not only does that make sense from a logistics perspective, it is also backed by the strong oral tradition that suggests this was the case. Then, the fact he returned to Rome two years later for a second time and was arrested and then executed, was confirmed by the ancient biblical historian, Eusebius, in his publication *History of the Church* in the year 313 AD (Eusebius 22:2).[127] The Apocryphal Acts of Peter also makes a similar assertion, and Paul's second letter to Timothy also strongly implies this is what happened.

- Why did Paul return to Rome after his trip to Hispania since Nero had launched his brutal persecution of Christians? We have many early Church documents as well as Church tradition that refer to Paul having been executed in Rome. We can therefore confirm with great certainty that Paul went back to Rome two years after he was set free. Why would he do that? We can only speculate but given that Paul had shown a deep commitment to his followers and to the communities he founded, he must have returned to find a way to protect the followers he had converted during his two years in house arrest in Rome.

- So, in addition to the above New Testament passages, and taking logic and historical facts into consideration, we also have three very important documents from very early in Christianity that mention Paul made the trip. In 96 AD, we have the direct reference of Clement-I, the third Bishop of Rome after Peter, confirming Paul made the trip when he wrote his letter to the Corinthians. Recognizing the fact that it was very likely Clement knew Paul on a first-hand basis, this evidence in particular is perhaps the most compelling. It is very difficult to simply discard it as not being relevant, as some historians have done.
- In addition, we have the Muratorian fragment from 160-170 AD that directly implies that he made the trip to Hispania. It provides the perspective that it was common knowledge in the early Christian communities that Paul traveled to Hispania, and therefore, the fragment documents the early Christian tradition, and belief, that he made the trip.
- We also have the apocryphal Acts of Peter, written in the mid-second century, and as such an important historical document of early Christianity, stating that Paul made the trip. It makes it clear that the early Christian community believed he made the trip, making this assertion consistent with the Muratorian fragment. Both documents make it clear that the early Christian communities of the second century believed Paul traveled to Hispania.
- Additionally, as covered in detail in Chapter-6, we have the writings of six Church "Doctors," so designated because of their highly respected writings and encyclicals, making references that Paul made the trip. All of these writings were within 400 years of

Paul's time, and all from biblical historians, which together support the early Church tradition that Paul made the trip.

- In addition to the above cited New Testament passages, the three very early church documents, and the writings from six Doctors of the Church, we also have the strong oral tradition from early Christian communities in Hispania. In Tarragona, there is a very strong tradition that Paul entered Hispania through Tarraco (Tarragona) and preached there. In southern Spain, we have the tradition that he preached in the Baetica province, today's Community of Andalucía. There, the strong tradition is that he visited the cities of Cordoba and Astigi (today's Ecija). There's also an ancient tradition that a Bishop named Gerontius, Bishop of Italica (Seville) towards the end of the first century AD, was a direct disciple of one of the Apostles. The only possibility of who that "Apostle" could be had to have been Paul. There are two other separate traditions. One is that Paul visited Salamanca and the other that he was in Augusta Emerita (today's Merida). If he had been in Italica, he likely traveled north from Italica, which was on the southern end of the Roman Via de la Plata and followed the Via north to Merida and then to Salamanca. All three cities were important cities on the roman Via de la Plata, and important land trade route in Hispania, and all three have strong oral traditions that cannot be ignored as simply being irrelevant.
- And finally, we have the strong tradition of the Eastern Orthodox Churches that have it as a fact that Paul did travel to Hispania. This tradition goes back to the first two centuries of Christianity, and since the Eastern Churches were founded by Paul, their knowledge and tradition that he made the trip must be taken very seriously, almost as a confirmation he made the trip.

This is a very impressive list of positive indications that support the premise Paul travelled to Hispania. With the preponderance of so much documentation, it is hard to give equal weight to the single contrary position by Pope Gelasius in the year 495 since he offered no evidence to the contrary. In fact, the evidence that does exist indicates that at that time Gelasius was dealing with so many conflicts with the Eastern Orthodox churches, that confirming Paul visited Hispania would not have been in Gelasius best interests.

A. Establishing the Steps of St. Paul in Hispania/Spain

Given the preponderance of evidence in favor of Paul having made the trip, the conclusion I have reached is therefore that Paul did in fact go to Hispania. It is almost certain he arrived in Tarraco, the Imperial capital of the Tarraconensis Province. Is it then possible to establish where precisely Paul preached while he was in Tarraco and other regions of Hispania?

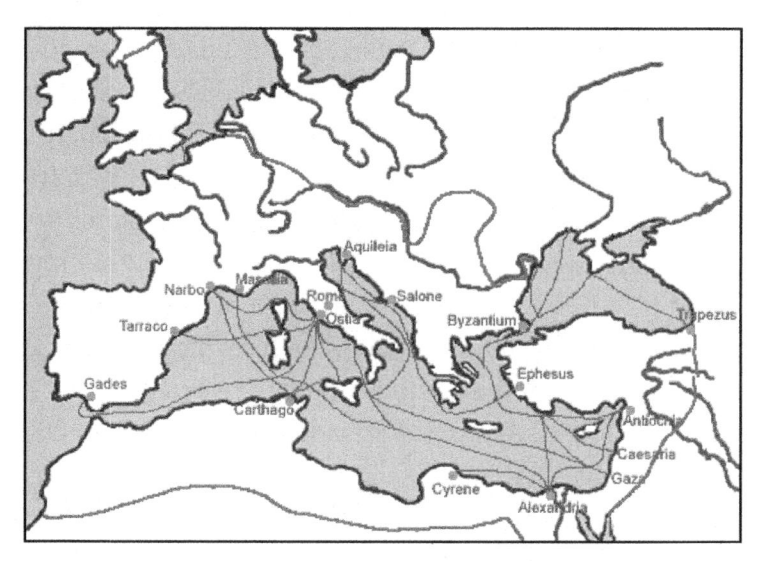

Fig. 46: Map of typical trading routes used by Romans, showing Tarraco as the main port of entry into Hispania[128]

Most historians agree that Paul would have entered Hispania using the normal sea route during Roman times, departing from the port of Ostia near Rome and arriving in Tarraco, the magnum port and fortress capital city of the Roman province Tarraconensis.

As illustrated in Fig. 46, the typical and safest trading route between Rome and Hispania would have ships departing from the Roman port of Ostia, crossing through the two fortified islands of Sardinia and Corsica, then arriving in the fortified city of Tarraco, which was then the Roman Imperial Capital of the very large Province of Tarraconensis.

Tarraco is today's Tarragona, 51 miles south of Barcelona, and Ostia, which is 15 miles west of Rome, served as Rome's principal port and harbor throughout antiquity.[129] This was a fairly safe four-day trip by ship.

Tarraco also had a Jewish community, and Paul surely must have been given that information during his two years in house arrest in Rome. So, this would almost certainly have been his entry point into Hispania.

Once there, Paul could begin his missionary trip in this important capital city. It is important to note here that Paul also followed a practice of preaching in the larger cities of the Empire, apparently trying to reach as many gentiles as possible, and Tarraco's characteristics definitely fit that description.

As to where in Tarraco Paul entered, we can certainly make a very good prediction of where in the city he would have entered and preached. This is explained in some detail in the next pages where a map of Tarraco is also provided (Fig. 47) in order to give a visual picture of Tarraco in Roman times.

As seen in Fig. 47, the Port of Tarraco lies at the southeastern tip of the walled-fortified city. Paul would have certainly entered through this busy port, which had a significant amount of trade and commercial activity all year round.

Fig. 47 also shows that the harbor area had a number of slips where ships coming from Rome could anchor. All around were numerous merchant shops involved in trade and commerce. These merchants would be moving goods into the open markets surrounding the port, as well as exporting products back to Rome.

Fig. 47: Depiction of Tarraco, around the year 100 AD.[130]

A bit further up you can see the local colonial forum buildings with an open-air space for large gatherings of the population. At the very top you can see the Temple of Augusto, and below it the Roman Circus, built after 70 AD, where chariots would race around its core center, many times in "death-to-the-end" races. To the right of the Roman Circus was the Amphitheater, where gladiators would also fight to the death. The Amphitheater is also where Bishop Fructuoso and his two deacons, Eulogio and Augurio, were burnt at the stake in the year 259 AD as part of the persecution launched by the Roman Emperor Valerian. (Note: the archeological ruins of the Forum, parts of the Circus, and most of the Amphitheater are still visible in today's Tarragona).

Paul surely recruited at least a couple of Roman followers while he was in house arrest to help him plan the trip to Hispania, which would have included landing first in Tarraco. There is also a strong early Christianity tradition coming out of the Baetica Province, that a certain disciple by the name of Hieroteo was recruited by Paul to travel with him to Hispania. Hieroteo was a merchant from the booming city of Astigi in the Baetica province, today's Ecija, around 55 miles south of Cordoba, the capital of the province at the time. While he was conducting commercial activities in the port city of Pafos in Cyprus, Hieroteo, heard Paul preaching and he became so enthralled by Paul's words that he was converted.[131]

That Paul was in Pafos and preached throughout Cyprus is well documented by Luke in Acts 13: 5-14. This tradition coming out of early Christianity in Ecija therefore matches closely the biblical versions of where Paul travelled according to Luke. That year would have been around 48.[132]

Hieroteo continued to follow Paul and quickly became one of Paul's most fervent disciples in Cyprus. The legend has it that when Paul reached Athens in Greece, he left Hieroteo there as the leader of that community. Eventually, Hieroteo was able to pass along the leadership to another local Christian convert to continue leading that community, so he was again able to join Paul in his travels.

Whether it was Hieroteo who joined Paul for the trip to Hispania, or Christian followers he converted while in Rome, they would have either known of or learned from their planning that there was a small but active Jewish community in Tarraco. From their planning, they would have learned that this community resided in the area known today as the Plaza of the Angels. This area is about one kilometer inland from the port, an easy walk for Paul and his team.

It is uncertain if the Jewish community of Tarraco had a synagogue at the time or if they met in the homes of individual Jewish members. As was his custom, Paul almost certainly visited those members as soon as he arrived and began speaking with them. Acts of the Apostles as well as Paul's letters document the fact that Paul typically received an initial willingness from members of Jewish communities to listen to what he had to say. Some were at first intrigued but would not be convinced by the potential that the Messiah had already arrived in the person of Jesus Christ. In some cases, these would turn harshly against Paul. Yet, others would accept Jesus as the Messiah and be converted.

Fig. 48: This image, also shown in Chapter-2, is an excellent representation of Paul speaking in a public forum[133]

After speaking to the members of the Jewish community, Paul would also quickly turn to the gentiles. Where in Tarraco would he have done that? His custom was to stand close to a large public place, like the local government forum, and loudly begin speaking to the crowds walking by.

Given his talent for attracting and converting new members to Christianity, Paul must have been a very powerful and eloquent speaker. Here we have to consider the Roman custom of having those with strong oratory skills speak from the steps of public places to crowds walking by. We can imagine Paul taking advantage of that custom and attracting dozens of listeners every time he spoke. He surely would have done that from the public places mentioned above, the ruins of which are still visible in Tarragona.

Paul also typically had success in finding someone from the communities he visited to allow him to stay with them and spend some time with that community. As was his practice, he would remain in that community a few months and then name a leader of that community to remain as the head of the new Christian Church he founded. He would then move on to another community to do the same.

So as far as Tarraco was concerned, we can be pretty certain that as soon as Paul arrived there, he walked up to the local Jewish community in the Plaza of the Angels to speak with its members. He certainly would have arranged to speak to them at the next Sabbath. To allow those wanting to speak to the congregation on subjects related to the religion was a well-established custom in Jewish communities.

Going up from the port to visit the Jewish community is almost certainly the path Paul would have taken on his first day in Tarraco. Soon after, he would have walked over to the colonial forum, and from one of its public steps, begin speaking to the crowds. This pattern of walking between the local Synagogue and the colonial forum would establish the first of "Paul's Steps of Hispania."

While in Tarraco, Paul must have also had the opportunity for his disciples to visit him there. In addition, because of his oratory skills and talent for conversions, there's a strong possibility he could have also converted new disciples in Tarraco to help him with his mission. Either his disciples, or Paul himself, would have then been able to travel to the Baetica Province, which was then the most important Roman province in Hispania.

It is important to note that the preferred route from Tarraco to the Baetica province was by sea, entering the province through the magnum military port of Urci, close to today's Almeria (see Fig. 49). The land route was not a particularly hospitable route to take and not the preferred route for merchants or travelers. From Urci, the Roman roads were well-established, taking travelers first to Acci, today's Guadix, which at the time was the town in the middle of two major commercial cross roads. One of those roads would take the traveler directly to Cordoba, the capital city of the province. Reaching the Baetica Province by landing in the port of Cartago Nova and then taking the land rout to the province was also a possibility, but this required travelers to take a much longer land route.

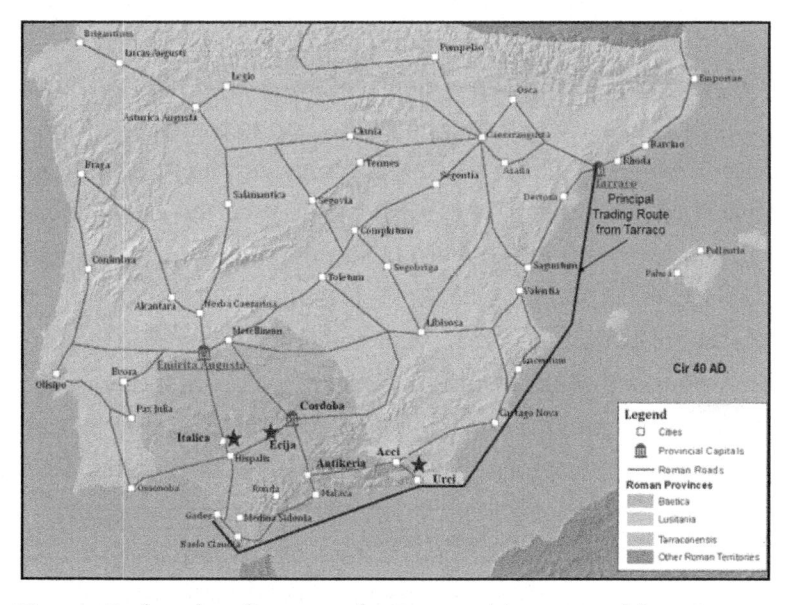

Fig. 49: Preferred trading route for Roman ships to travel from Tarraco down to the Baetica Province, entering through Urci and reaching Acci, a major trading cross-roads in the Province.

As already mentioned, only fifty-five kilometers south of Cordoba was Astigi, which as mentioned in Chapter-6, has a very strong tradition of Paul having preached there. And only 95 kilometers south of Astigi, was Italica, next to Hispalis, today's Seville, where there is also a strong tradition Paul travelled there.

Therefore, the strong oral traditions of where Paul visited also make sense from a geographic and logistics perspective. He would have planted the seeds to what would grow to be the most important Christian region in Hispania, and one of the most important in the known Christian world of that time.

B. Additional Comments on the Possibility St. James Also Visited Hispania

At this point it is important to address the possibility that Saint James (SanTiago) also visited Hispania. I should make the assertion here that having Paul travel to Hispania on a missionary trip should not be seen as contradicting the tradition that St. James also visited Hispania by the year 40AD.

Many biblical historians believe that the evidence strongly indicates St. James did not make that trip and that this legend is based on conflicting oral traditions. However, as mentioned in the Introduction to this book, that tradition is so strong that I do not want to negate it in any way, and in fact, I believe it needs to be respected. I believe it is a tradition that should be embraced given the fact that for the Camino of Santiago (the Way of St. James) to become such an important Christian pilgrimage, it must have had the force of the Holy Spirit behind it.

By the same token, and just as important, I believe the evidence that Paul traveled to Hispania should be embraced. There is just too much evidence to make any other conclusion. The fact is that the tradition of St. James places him in the northern regions of Hispania, but the evidence surrounding Paul places him in Tarraco and in the Southern Baetica region of Hispania. Therefore, the possible visit of St. James to Hispania's northern regions should not contradict the conclusion we have made in this book that Paul made a missionary trip there.

As to who was responsible for planting the seeds of Christianity on the peninsula, there is also an overwhelming amount of evidence that Christianity grew and flourish in the places where Paul visited. Adding to the evidence presented in this book is the oral traditions of the local churches and the Eastern Orthodox Christian churches. It is therefore hard to refute the premise that it was Paul who planted those seeds.

C. Purpose of this chapter

The purpose of this chapter was therefore to summarize all the evidence presented in this book indicating Paul conducted his missionary trip to Hispania, a trip that he considered of the highest priority. Since the evidence is so strong, I make the unequivocal conclusion and assertion in this chapter that Paul indeed made the trip.

Given this conclusion, I have combined historical facts with common sense logic to propose another very important assertion: the "Steps" Paul must have taken in Hispania. He would have arrived through the Port of Tarraco, preached in the city for some time to both the Jewish community there as well as to the gentile community. He later would have travelled down to the Baetica Province. There, the strong oral tradition places him in Ecija (55 kilometers southwest of Cordoba), and Italica (10 kilometers from Hispalis (today's Seville). There's additional tradition he preached in Emerita Augusta (today's Merida) and Salamanca.

By establishing the "Steps of St. Paul in Hispania," it is hoped that many in the future many will follow his path.

CHAPTER 10

FINAL COMMENTS AND CONCLUSIONS

With so much research material and documentation that has been presented in this book, it is imperative to provide a final summary of how this information led to the conclusions presented herein.

I've been careful to document and provide credible sources for every major point raised and conclusions reached. In addition, I've interviewed and provided the personal input from a number of biblical historians, archeologist, university professors, priest-historians, and even an archbishop in Spain—who is also a historian—to validate those conclusions.

That said, given the subject matter of this book, some of the conclusions reached are impossible to prove. We can, however, provide the evidence and historical information discovered, present a detailed analysis of that evidence, provide a discussion on the interpretation of that analysis, and finally, as researchers "connect the dots" in order to scientifically reach valid conclusions.

That's what I have done with the material presented in this book. The information provided throughout the book is therefore completely backed by research findings from highly distinguished biblical historians. It includes well documented archival materials from early and current church history, augmented by the testimony from highly respected sources that I personally interviewed. As a result, I feel it is an important work that should be disseminated and discussed by those interested in religious studies, especially as it pertains to Christianity.

In addition to presenting very compelling information that Paul made a missionary trip to Hispania, I have also provided the historical evidence that confirms Christianity grew in Hispania to a very advance level by the end of the third century. Additional evidence has been presented to support arguments that Hispania ended up having an enormous positive impact in the evolution of Christianity in the centuries that followed Paul's trip. That impact, and those developments, took place first during early Christianity, followed by the Middle Ages, and later during the evangelization of the Americas. When connected, these provide a very powerful and convincing set of facts on how critically important Spain has been to Christianity.

We therefore summarize here the findings and conclusions presented in the book, including the fact Paul travelled to Hispania, as well as the very compelling research findings that encapsulate the importance of Hispania/Spain to the evolution of Christianity:

A. Paul Travelled to Hispania

With the evidence that has been presented throughout this book, it is hard to reach any other conclusion other than Paul **did conduct** his very high priority missionary trip to Hispania. He would have entered through the imperial capital of Tarraco, spent a couple of months there, and for sure left a leader in charge of that newly founded Christian community. That leader would almost certainly have been from the local Tarraco community, but he also likely left one of his disciples from Rome to provide additional guidance.

Paul then travelled down to the Baetica province. During Paul's missionary years, the Baetica Province had one of the highest population densities in the Roman Empire, basically all of them gentiles, with only a couple of small Jewish communities. The large gentile population would have positioned Hispania among the highest priorities for Paul to want to preach there and to spread the Word of Jesus to its population.

Keep in mind that Paul saw his very specific mission the conversion of gentiles to this new religion. As mentioned in Chapter-2, Paul himself testified this mission was given to him directly by Jesus, and therefore, the reason why preaching there was such a high priority for Paul. It is the main premise of this book that it was Paul's enormous talent for converting individuals, establishing new church communities, naming leaders as bishops, and leaving them with strict rules to follow, the reason Christian communities in the Baetica Province grew to be perhaps the largest in the then Christian world by the end of the third century.

As most historians have concluded, it must have taken a very charismatic person, one who was also a high Christian authority, to have planted the seeds that led to such rapid growth of Christianity in Hispania. That person, I'm declaring in this book, was the Apostle Paul.

B. Is the Council of Elvira (Granada), which was Enormously Important to Early Christianity, an Indication Paul Founded Christianity in Hispania?

In Chapter-7, I presented the facts surrounding the Council of Elvira. This was the first Christian Council in the history of the Church in which rules and norms (canons) for Christians to lead their lives were established. In that chapter, I documented that it took place in the Roman city of Iliberis (today's Granada Spain) sometime between the years 300 to 304 AD. Iliberis was located next to the Elvira Mountain range, and that's the reason why it is most often mentioned as the Council of Elvira.

There were 19 bishops present at the Council, together with representatives from 37 Christian communities, all of them from Hispania. This was the first Christian council documented in Church history where an extensive number of strict norms and rules were established for Christians to conduct their lives, 81 such norms to be exact.

The fact that this Council was held in Hispania is an indication of how advanced Christian concepts had evolved as compared to other early Christian communities around the world. This Council produced some of the most important tenets and norms for Christians to lead their lives, most of which are still in practice today. There were no representatives at this Council from Rome, nor from any of the churches in Northern Africa, which would indicate the Churches of Hispania felt they had the independent authority themselves to establish such strict rules.

This is a critical point: the churches in Hispania did not seek approval or authority to publish such strict rules. They felt they had the authority to do so without permission from any other Christian authority at the time. There was no one there from any other major Christian region: Rome, Antioch, Alexandria or Jerusalem. This is a conclusion that I have not found from any other historian.

The critical point here is that these churches obviously had such a strong tradition, that the roots of their Christian beliefs must have been planted by a direct apostle to Jesus. The 19 bishops that signed the canons that came out of the Council had to have known that they were the first to come up with such rules and norms for them to live by. There is no documented history of any other early Christian community coming up with such strict rules.

So, the fact they did not seek permission from any other Church authority to establish these rules clearly indicates they felt they had that authority bestowed on them by some highly respected early

Christian authority. This fact positioned the Church in Hispania as one the most advanced in early Christianity, and all indications are that it became so without any direct influence from other early Christian communities or Christian authority.

The Council of Elvira points to the fact that right from the beginning, the Church of Hispania was founded by a very high Christian authority with the power to engender a sense of authority and independence from other Christian hierarchy. The only individual who had the power to bestow that authority, who as confirmed in this book, was documented to have travelled to Hispania, was the Apostle Paul.

C. Bishop Osio of Cordoba Emerged as One of the Most Important Early Christian Theologians

Also discussed in Chapter-7, Bishop Osio of Cordoba, who had an important role in the Council of Elvira in 302/304 AD, was the bishop that presided over the Council of Nicaea in 325 AD. The Council of Nicaea is today considered the most important council in the history of the Church, with the Nicene Creed as one of its most important outcomes. It was convened by Emperor Constantine around ten years after Christianity was ratified as a legal religion. There were 318 bishops from Church communities all over the Christian world gathered to establish the theological tenets and guidelines for the Christian Church.

An immensely important point detailed in Chapter-7 is that Emperor Constantine chose Bishop Osio to preside over the Council of Nicaea. Osio's role in presiding over the Council highlights the advanced level of Christian thought that must have existed in Hispania. The fact Constantine chose Osio of Cordoba, and not the Bishop of Rome, nor the Bishop of Constantinople, nor any other bishop, would indicate that Constantine must have believed that in Cordoba, and therefore in Hispania, the concepts of Christianity had advanced to the highest levels of Christianity.

When considering this argument, keep in mind that Christianity was very splintered at that time and there was no central theological institution like we have today. It is important to take into account that it wasn't until the Council of Nicaea in 325 AD that the four Christian Patriarchies of early Christianity were established: Rome, Alexandria, Antioch, and Jerusalem. Rome was officially set as the episcopal see of the Patriarchy that included Italy and all the western regions from Rome. The other patriarchal cities were established as the episcopal sees for the regions representing the eastern Christian churches. Each see was given equal responsibility for the episcopal supervision of their region, and the Bishop of each as the religious leader, or Patriarch, oversaw all other bishops in the region. Later, in the Council of Chalcedon in the year 451, the City of Constantinople was also added, making it five Patriarchies, which was then referred to as the Pentarchy.

These five Patriarchates essentially remained in existence until the year 1054, when the schism between the Eastern Orthodox Churches and the western churches of Rome took place.

Going back then to the Council of Nicaea, it was here that Rome was given the designation of "Primus Inter Pares," or "First Among Equals." This was done in recognition of its role as the heart of the Roman Empire. It was also in recognition that there were some bishops who had begun to express the idea that the direct line of bishops that followed Peter, as the first bishop of Rome and the Vicar of Christ, should position Rome slightly higher than the others. However, the concept that the Bishop of Rome should be bestowed with the primacy over all of Christianity, did not start to become more prevalent until the fifth century. This concept, which led eventually to the term of "Pope," began to be more aggressively pushed by the Bishops of Rome around the year 500 AD.

The point to be made here is that in the first 300 years, the church was very splintered, with each region evolving their Christian faith and beliefs, limited in large part by discussions of their regional Christian hierarchy and leaders. They evolved in an almost "regionally enclosed" existence. Therefore, the Council of Elvira in Hispania, which took place between the years 300-304 AD, must have stood out at the time since its bishops came together to discuss and debate the tenets of the faith and of how Christians should lead their lives. The fact that the council took place, and that its results and proceedings became well-known across Christendom, must have been the reason that it also became known to Emperor Constantine.

It's hard to imagine any other reason as to why Constantine would have known of Osio. As mentioned in Chapter-7, Constantine's father, Constantius, had ruled the northwestern tetrarchy that included Brittany and France. Constantine inherited his tetrarchy after Constantius died, and it wasn't until the year 312 AD that Constantine won in battle the tetrarchy of Maximian, the Roman Emperor who ruled over the tetrarchy that included Hispania and Italy. It was in that battle that Constantine received the message that he would defeat Maximian under the symbol of the Christian Cross.

Therefore, Constantine did not accept Christianity as a legitimate religion until 312 AD, and he would only then begin to get to know the Christian roots of Hispania.

Why would Constantine, shortly after his conversion, choose Osio, the Bishop of Cordoba, to become his spiritual advisor and later to preside over the Council of Nicaea? The logical conclusion, or perhaps the only conclusion we can reach, is that the importance to early Christianity of the Council of Elvira and that Osio had been its leader must have become well-known throughout the Christian world. This is about the only logical conclusion we can reach as to why Constantine would select the bishop from a region and a religion he was just beginning to learn about.

Nothing else makes sense. Constantine did not go seek out the Bishop of Rome, or of Alexandria, or of Antioch, or any other bishop. He selected Osio from Cordoba, Hispania.

There is an additional logical conclusion we can reach from this fact. It is that the Christian Church of Hispania, with the results from the Council of Elvira, must have been considered as being very advanced in the tenets and beliefs of Christianity.

Consequently, as presented and explained in the Introduction and throughout this book, Hispania/Spain has definitely held a unique place in history for how vital its impact has been on the early evolution, later protection, and subsequent expansion of Christianity. There is no doubt that the churches of Jerusalem, Antioch, Alexandria and Rome, were critical in the early evolution during the first century of Christianity. But the results from the Council of Elvira indicates that in Hispania, and particularly in the Baetica province, there had to have been someone plant the roots of Christianity there. This person had to have had equal weight to those who planted the roots in these other churches. The overwhelming evidence points to that "someone" being the Apostle Paul.

Logic would then point to the fact the Council of Elvira must have become known around early Christian circles as an extremely important council in establishing how Christians should lead their lives. Since Osio convened it, and since there is evidence he was a masterful speaker, Constantine must have used that information to decide in favor of Osio presiding over the Council of Nicaea. Therefore, the most important "outcome" coming out of the most important council in the history of the Church, the Nicene Creed, was overseen and most likely greatly influenced by Osio, and undoubtedly, also by the other Bishops from Hispania present.

Again, this points to the tremendous importance of Hispania in the evolution of Christianity. This then leads to the question of who founded Christianity in Hispania, since the tenets of the religion and how Christians should lead their lives evolved without outside influence from any other "authority" of the Christian Church. It is the premise of this book that it was the Apostle Paul who bestowed such independent authority on the Church of Hispania.

D. The Critical Role Played by the Early Visigoth Christian Kings in the Recovery of Their Lands from the Muslims Could Have Saved Christianity from Extinction

As covered in Chapter-8, over the first seven centuries AD, the Christian kings and people of Hispania had developed a tremendous commitment to Christianity, including the veneration of the Virgin Mary. However, after the sudden invasion by Islamic forces in 711 AD, in only nine years the Muslims successfully took most of Hispania, with the exception of a small section in the north known as Asturias.

Beginning in the year 722 with Pelayo of Asturias, who would be proclaimed Prince of Asturias, that commitment to Christianity was crucial in the re-conquest of the territory that had been Christian Hispania. This effort by the Christian kings and people of Hispania highlights the critical importance of Spain to the overall evolution of Christianity, but perhaps more importantly, to its survival. Had the Christian people of Hispania and their kings not fought to recover their lands in order to reinstate their Christian culture and Christian faith, it is very likely that not only Spain, but most of Europe, would have succumbed to Islamic rule.

It is a reality that by stopping the advancing Muslim forces and later recovering their lost Christian lands, the make-up of Europe and the evolution of Christianity would have been very different if not for the Christians of Hispania. The logical conclusion of an Islamic Europe together with the rest of Islamic countries would have led to the likely eradication of Christianity. It is important to note here, that during the Middle Ages there were dozens of kingdoms created and defeated all over Europe and the Middle East, including both Christian and Islamic. However, the recovery of Christian territory by the Christian people of Hispania was pivotal in the survival of the religion.

E. Evangelization of the Americas

And speaking of the evolution of Christianity, the two countries that originally made up Hispania, Spain an Portugal, conducted the most impressive expansion of Christianity with the evangelization of the Americas. Spain was mostly responsible for that expansion, but Portugal also had an important part with the evangelization of Brazil. By the time the British pilgrims arrived 130 years later, Spain had already spread Christianity throughout most of South America, Central America and large parts of North America, including Mexico, California, Texas, and six other current states. Portugal led a strong Christianization of Brazil, which is today the Latin American country with the largest number of Christians. Latin American countries as a group today represent the largest block of Christians in the world, and it was the original evolution of Christianity from what was then Hispania that led to this fact.

F. Final Comments

Based on all the above, is there any doubt Hispania/Spain played a uniquely important role, perhaps even the most important one together with Rome, in the early evolution, later protection and eventually the largest expansion of Christianity? Especially when compared to other regions of the world?

Interestingly, Spain also had an immense influence in the evolution of thought and philosophies involving Islam and Judaism. During the second half of the "Middle Ages," Al-Andalus, which is the region of Hispania that had been taken over by the Islamic caliphate, engendered some of the most important religious philosophers of these two religions. We have included in Appendix-A a summary of the positive impact Al-Andalus had on both Islam and Judaism. As examples, Maimonides for Judaism and Averroes for Islam are highlighted, who together with other Middle-Age philosophers from this region of the world, expanded the discourse on the tenets of their religion.

These three monotheistic religions, all three of which have their roots to Abraham, the first Hebrew Patriarch, evolved through a very intense level of discourse and debates by philosophers throughout the ages. Hispania and Al-Andalus, regions that became mostly

Spain but also Portugal, were deeply central to the evolution of the concepts surrounding the three religions.

In providing final comments and conclusions, I am humbled by the fact that what started ten years ago as a simple interest to look into whether the Apostle Paul had been in Spain, kept expanding and growing to the point that not only Paul, but many other elements of the importance of Spain to Christianity evolved from the research. Now that I am this deep into this project, my next set of initiatives will be to conduct additional research in the Vatican Archives and in the Escorial (Spain) Biblical Library.

I have come to the realization that there has to be an obscure set of documents that will shed light into Paul's missionary trip to Hispania. There's just too much information that points to that reality. To reach this conclusion, I've had to connect a number of what appear to be on the surface independent and unrelated sets of research elements. We can understand why the Church in Spain and Rome might not want to make a definitive statement on Paul's trip to Hispania, but a simple declaration that new evidence points to the strong probability that he did, would help clear this issue.

It's also important to put in perspective that there have been thousands of books and documents published that analyzed every aspect of Paul's life. It would literally be impossible for me, or anyone, to have reviewed all the existing literature available. I have, however, done a fairly comprehensive level of research of books and documents that focus on Paul's trips. I have also spoken with, and interviewed, a number of subject-matter experts who have added a significant amount of information to my research.

With the extensive amount of research elements I have compiled, and with the new relevant information that has evolved from that research, this book appears to be the first that sets the actual "Steps of St. Paul in Hispania."

This book brings a new perspective on two important points that I believe have been lost in history: that the Apostle Paul conducted a missionary trip to Hispania, and that Hispania/Spain has had an enormous level of importance in the evolution, protection and expansion of Christianity. I totally recognize that there are other opinions by respected researchers so hopefully this book will continue to extend the discussion.

I am therefore making a definitive statement in this book that the Apostle Paul is responsible for planting the seeds of Christianity in Hispania. We are aware of the very strong tradition that St. James could have been responsible for bringing Christianity to Hispania. That tradition is not supported by historical facts, although I strongly respect it since it has led to such an important pilgrimage for Christians since the IX century. On the other hand, the evidence and oral traditions that Paul conducted a missionary trip to Hispania go back to the first and second centuries, and continued for the following three centuries.

Therefore, until someone can come along and prove that the research presented in this book is erroneous, and also prove that Paul never made it to Hispania, I'll continue to propose that at the very least, Paul fulfilled his high priority missionary trip to Hispania.

That said, I believe there should be room in our beliefs, traditions and documented research to respect both positions: that St. James conducted a missionary trip to the northern regions of Hispania, and that St. Paul made his missionary trip to the southern regions of Hispania.

It is hoped that the conclusions presented here will become part of the future discourse on the tremendously important role Hispania played in the evolution of Christianity and that the Apostle Paul made a missionary trip there.

With the additional research I plan to conduct in the Vatican and in the Escorial (Spain) Biblical Library, there will hopefully be additional information that helps uncover why Paul's trip to Spain has remained unconfirmed by the Catholic Church. Could there have been a reason to hide that information?

Stay tuned...

Appendix

THE HISTORICAL IMPORTANCE OF THE REGION OF AL-ANDALUS IN THE EVOLUTION OF PHILOSOPHICAL CONCEPTS OF ISLAM AS WELL AS JUDAISM

As I continued my research surrounding Spain and the evolution of Christianity, another separate and very intriguing set of insights evolved. I began to realize that Hispania was somehow a place that engendered and produced some of the top philosophers and religious leaders of their times, especially in regard to the three Abrahamic religions of Christianity, Judaism and Islam. I was uncovering information beyond what even most current Spaniards knew about their own history. Hispania's influence was not just on the evolution of Christian precepts and beliefs. There were also several very important philosophers that came out of Hispania that had a profound influence in the advancement of precepts surrounding Judaism as well as Islam.

I therefore felt it was important to include in this book, at least as an Appendix, a summary that highlighted the significant impact Hispania had during the Middle Ages in the evolution of tenets for Judaism and Islam. This literally positions Hispania in a unique place in history since outside of the Palestine region, there are only a couple of other regions in the world that had such an impact over the three religions.

To summarize, the book focused on the importance of Hispania in the evolution of Christianity, and in particular in the early evolution of Christian tenets, as evident by the Council of Elvira in 302 AD. The importance of Bishop Osio of Cordoba, as well as the advance concepts of Christianity that developed in Hispania, had a major impact in the results coming out of the Council of Nicaea, the most important council in Church history.

In the following pages, the focus will then be on a quick summary of Judaism and Islam in Hispania, beginning first with the Jewish presence in Hispania and the evolution of Jewish philosophical concepts there, followed by a similar focus on Islam.

It's important to first document the fact that for centuries prior to the Roman occupation of Hispania, and through its current history, there have been numerous Jewish communities settled in Hispania. Even after the expulsion of Jewish and Muslim families following the re-conquest of Granada, many Jewish families remained and practiced Judaism in secret.

As highlighted in Fig. 10 from Chap. 1, and shown here again as Figure 1 of the Apendix, there were multiple Phoenician colonies established in the southern part of Hispania prior to the Roman occupation in the 3rd Century BC. Since Jewish sailors would partner with Phoenicians, small groups of Jewish families also settled in with the Phoenicians.

Although small, these Jewish communities were already established when the three major Jewish expulsions from Rome and Jerusalem by the Roman Emperors took place in the first Century

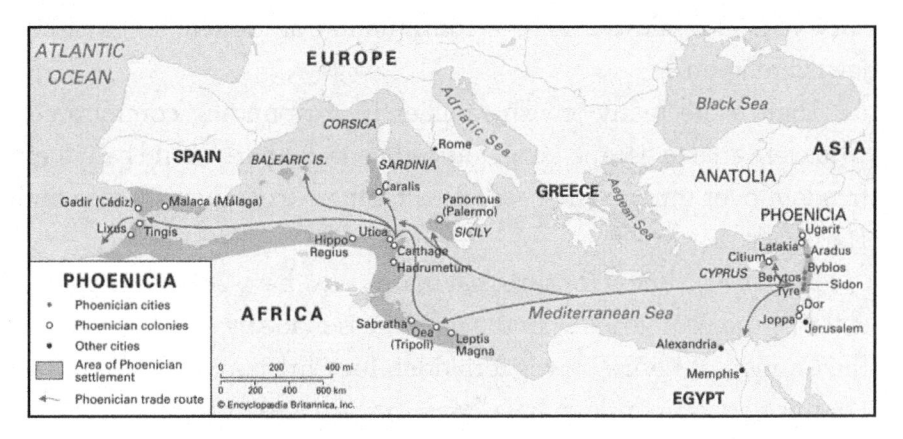

Fig 1 (Fig. 10 from Ch. 1): From the time of King Solomon to around 300 BC, Phoenician and Greek Colonies, were established to control trade routes. Map shows Phoenicians, with Jewish sailors as partners, established colonies in southern regions of the Iberia peninsula, known as Tarshish during that time, which later became known as Hispania

AD. Those three expulsions are documented in history as follows: in the year 19 AD, the expulsion from Rome by the Emperor Tiberius; in the year 49 AD, a second expulsion from Rome by the Emperor Claudius; and the worst of all, in the year 70 AD, the destruction of the Second Temple and most of Jerusalem by Emperor Vespasian, who left his son, the Roman General Titus, in charge of the destruction. Fig. 2 of this Appendix illustrates the horror that must have taken over the population with total destruction of the City and the Temple.

Hispania would therefore have been a possibility for Jewish families to settle there during those expulsions. Not only were there Jewish communities already established there, but the region was relatively friendly since Roman governors in this region were not as brutal as their Emperors.

After the destruction of Jerusalem, which resulted in the destruction of the Temple, it is estimated that as many as 100,000 Jews were sent into exile, with many sold as slaves. A few of the Jewish religious leaders survived and the Torah Learning Center at Yavneh also survived. This allowed for the continuation of the teachings of the Jewish religion.[134]

There were many Jewish families in surrounding communities who were able to escape Israel altogether and others would gain their freedom over time. Some headed east, others to Turkey, Greece and North Africa.

But we also know for sure that many must have gone to Hispania since by the year 300 AD, in the references made by the 81 canons of the Council of Elvira, it was forbidden for Christians to marry Jews. For this very strict rule to have been in place and documented, there must have been a significant community of Jews already in Hispania.

This would imply that over a couple of centuries both communities of Jewish and Christians, had considerably increased in Hispania.

Fig. 2: Destruction of the Second Temple of Jerusalem, Francesco Hayez, 1867

Continuing with the growth of Christianity in Hispania, it has been well documented that by the year 500 AD the Christian

Visigoths were starting to consolidate power throughout Hispania, and by the end of the VI Century would control all of Hispania. They set some very strict rules prohibiting Jews from practicing their faith in public. As explained in previous chapters, these very strict rules created a heightened level of resentment by the Jews towards the Visigoth rulers.

As was detailed in Chapter-8, Jewish leaders turned against the Christian Visigoths and helped the Muslims invade Hispania in the year 711, which led to the establishment of the Caliphate of Al Andalus. The goodwill that created, led the Muslim kings to provide concessions to Jewish communities throughout Al Andalus, and that allowed them to practice in their synagogues for the next four centuries. The result was that Jewish communities were able to continue growing, especially in Cordoba, the capital of Al Andalus.

The reason this point is important is because the region of Hispania would have had the presence of Jewish communities for many centuries following the destruction of the Temple. These Jewish communities would have had their leaders, rabbis and philosophers living there. Given their separation from the rest of the Jewish world, these philosophers would have been discussing and debating sacred scriptures in some level of isolation, and this would allow for discourse that led to better understanding of the meanings of their religion.

Over the next 400 years that followed the Muslim invasion of Hispania, Jewish communities grew and prospered in the region of Al-Andalus. It was during this time that a small but very important group of Jewish philosophers emerged in Cordoba.

Fig. 3: Statue of Maimonides, taken by Dr. Figueredo, in the Jewish Quarter of Cordoba

The most famous of these Jewish philosophers was Rabbi Moses ben Maimon, commonly known as Maimonides, who was born in the Muslim Caliphate of Cordoba in the year 1135.[135] Maimonides had considerable influence on Jewish thought and the evolution of precepts related to Judaism. His works caused considerable controversy, especially concerning the relations between reason and divine revelation.

His writings and philosophical perspectives on Judaism as a "revealed religion" have had a profound impact and continue to be debated even today. We don't pretend that it is possible to provide expert commentary here on such a distinguished philosopher, but an example of this were his writings on the Law of Repentance, in the *Mishneh Torah*. The *Mishneh Torah* provided extensive commentary on the Talmud and consists of fourteen books, each covering one subject, and subdivided into sections and chapters. It is the only Medieval-era work that details all of Jewish observance, including those laws that are only applicable when the Holy Temple is in existence, and remains still today an important work in Judaism.[136] Maimonides' intention when he wrote it was to make it accessible to as many readers as possible, instead of only having major scholars as the only ones able to understand it.[137]

So why did Maimonides have such an important impact on Judaism in the XII century when this was a religion that had been in existence and studied for over two thousand years before?

To answer this question, we actually need to go back to what happened after the destruction of the Second Temple in 70 AD. We need to understand that the Romans not only destroyed the physical Temple, they also destroyed the "seat of knowledge" of the Jewish Nation.

In the process, they killed and murdered many of their very distinguished Jewish philosophers, rabbis, and leaders, thereby eliminating a large portion of those who had knowledge of the tenets of Judaism, and how their religion could be interpreted and understood. Although the Torah Learning Center at Yavneh and a few of their leaders survived, there was a major dispersion of Jews to areas all over the Roman Empire.

The surviving rabbis and Jewish leaders were now facing a new reality, Judaism without a Temple. Not only had they lost the concept of a geographic nation, Judea, they also lost their national center for studies and philosophical debates on religions concepts surrounding Judaism. To make matters worse, the Jewish Nation found itself one more time facing a massive diaspora. Their interaction with their faith during the subsequent centuries occurred at a very local level, with some exchanges of thought taking place in a very limited way by the most respected rabbis. Through debate, they went back to the concepts that the Jewish Nation was created from the ancestors of Abraham himself, and the notion that there had to be a geographic "nation," although very important, was not critical to the religion.

Shortly after the destruction of Jerusalem, rabbinic discourse and philosophical religious concepts started to be written down and kept as versions of the laws that needed to be followed. Jewish leaders realized that the previous tradition of keeping an oral-base religion was not practical anymore and started to write down the laws and instructions for Jewish life. These became what made up the Talmud, and it became critically important to Jewish life after the destruction of Jerusalem and the Temple. It forged the concept that Jewish law bounded them together despite the fact they were dispersed all over the world. The Talmud was therefore extensively studied and discussed, eventually becoming the most important interpretation and clarification of commandments in the Torah as Divine Revelation[138].

Up until the Middle Ages and the time of Maimonides, there were theological debates and discussions on the philosophical tenets implied by the Talmud as they related to the Torah. Maimonides had become an expert on scriptures and the Talmud and was a highly respected judge on legal official issues related to Judaism when he later moved to Egypt, becoming a physician in the Muslim court there.

There is no doubt that throughout the first millennial AD, Hispania and Al Andalus, had a growing and expanding set of Jewish communities that allowed for the continued discussion and evolution of the tenets of Judaism. Maimonides represents the best example of how the philosophical discourse and debates that were taking place in Al Andalus had a lasting impact on the religion.

Maimonides has remained an important philosopher and key figure in Jewish religious tradition. His philosophical positions have offered extensive guidance on matters of Jewish law and Jewish life. Although there has been significant debate over the years on whether the central role ascribed to "reason" by Maimonides conflicts with Judaism as a revelation-based religious tradition, it has been well established that he had a major influence on its interpretation.

And as it relates to Islam, its presence in Al Andalus for over 700 years resulted in a number of major philosophical edicts concerning the interpretations of the Quran. Beginning in the year 756 with the

Emir Abd al-Rahman-I, who created the Emirate of Cordoba under the Umayyad Dynasty, and continuing until the surrender of King Boabdil of the Kingdom of Granada in 1492, Islamic philosophers from Hispania had a major influence on the religion.

In fact, the term, "The Golden Age of Islam" is used most often when referring to the Caliphate of Cordoba for the period between the X and XII centuries, although in a larger context for all of Islam, it covered the IX through the XIII century. Beginning with the leadership of Abd-ar-Rhaman III in 929 after he created the Caliphate of Cordoba, this period saw a major surge in philosophical thought for both Judaism as well as Islam.

The reason for the advancement of Judaism under an Islamic caliphate is that Abd-ar-Rhaman recognized not only that the Jewish leaders had helped provide information that defeated the Visigoth Christians two centuries before, but he also saw the talent they provided in medicine and in managing the assets of the caliphate.

There were therefore major advancements during these two centuries in religion, in medicine, in the sciences, in mathematics, and in the arts and culture. Many global historians have actually documented that the Caliphate of Cordoba during the period between the years 929 and 1030 was considered a separate country. It was considered the most culturally advanced country in the world with a population of 2 million, and the Capital City of Cordoba with a population of 500,000[139].

Perhaps the most emblematic building that still stands from this period is the "Great Mosque" of Cordoba, with its first phase built in the VIII century over the remains of the Visigoth Basilica of San Vicente.

This basilica was destroyed by the Muslim leadership in order to build the Mosque. There were several extensions of the Mosque until the city was recovered in the year 1236 by the Christian King Fernando III who converted it into a Cathedral. Of great historical interest is the fact that King Fernando was so impressed with the building and

Fig. 4: Abd-ar-Rahman III and his court in Medina Azahara Painting: Dionisio Baixeras Verdaguer 1932

what it represented to its citizens, that he decided to not destroy the Mosque. Instead he built several altars in its center and converted it into the Cathedral of Cordoba.

For those who have this as an e-book, you can see the amazing process of its construction here: https://www.youtube.com/watch?v=1Q2QoWyXSzM

Fig. 5: Illustrates the current Cathedral in the middle of what used to be the "Great Mosque" of Cordoba

UNESCO has designated Cordoba's Cathedral as a World Heritage Site. Today it is referred to often as the Cathedral Mesquite at Cordoba, and as such it is a unique building in the world. UNESCO used the following criteria in its designation[140]:

- **Criterion (i):** The Great Mosque of Cordoba, with its dimensions and the boldness of its interior, which were never imitated, make it a unique artistic creation
- **Criterion (ii):** Despite its uniqueness, the mosque of Cordoba has exercised a considerable influence on western Muslim art from the 8th century. It influenced the development as well of "Neo-Moresque" styles of the 19th century.
- **Criterion (iii):** The Historic Centre of Córdoba is the highly relevant testimony to the Caliphate of Cordoba (929-1031): this city—which, it is said, enclosed 300 mosques and innumerable palaces—was the rival of Constantinople and Baghdad.
- **Criterion (iv):** It is an outstanding example of the religious architecture of Islam

When we see the inside design of the Cathedral we can clearly pick-up the use of Muslim architectural features such as the arches and ceiling designs (Figure 6).

Fig. 6: Inside look at one small section of the Mesquite at Cordoba

During the period the building was a Mesquite, one amazing and unique element is that after the last expansion, it could hold as many as 30,000 individuals inside for prayers and other activities.

Just as with Judaism, the 500 years of the territory known as Al-Andalus sprouted a number of philosophers that probed deeply into the religious tenets of Islam. Perhaps one of the more famous was the Cordoba born and raised Ahmad Ibn Rushd, better known by the Latinized "Averoes" (1126-1198). Although we don't pretend to be an expert on the evolution of Islamic thought, it is well established that he was considered a great Muslim philosopher during his time even though some of his writings were controversial. He was responsible for planting the seed and influencing the rise of secular thought in Western Europe[141].

Fig. 7: Ahmad Ibn Rushd, Averroes, Islam Philosopher from Cordoba. Painting by Andrea di Bonaiuto, XIV Century

In addition to being an Islamic philosopher and theologian, Averroes analyzed and wrote a number of thesis on medieval sciences including medicine, astronomy, physics and celestial mechanics. He was known for his high level of intelligence as well as his analytical skills. Although highly regarded as a legal scholar of the Maliki School of Islamic Law, Averroes' philosophical ideas were considered controversial in a number of Muslim circles. Whereas other well-known philosophers believed that any natural phenomenon occurred only because God willed it to happen, Averroes argued that any such phenomena followed natural laws that God created[142].

Averroes is but one of many philosophers that were born and raised in Al-Andalus. Beginning in the VIII century, with the formation of the Emirate of Cordoba, each Emir, and later Caliphs, would bring to their courts highly respected Islamic philosophers, scientists, mathematicians, doctors and scholars in all disciplines. Another example is Caliph Al-Ma'mun in the IX Century, who introduced ancient Greek philosophy into the region of Al Andalus.[143]

The above discussion on how Judaism as well as Islam had great moments of advancements show that they flourished during various periods of time in Hispania. This is an important historical element that makes Hispania a unique region of the world.

We hope that the evidence presented in this appendix along with the analysis and discussion presented in the book, provides the reader the clear picture that Hispania/Spain was very influential beyond just the evolution of Christianity, having also had a strong influence in the discussion and emerging tenets of Judaism and Islam.

END NOTES

1. Mark Damen USU History Faculty, http://www.usu.edu/markdamen/1320Hist&Civ/slides/13xity/mapspreadofxity.jpg, retrieved January 10, 2010
2. Fr. Manuel Martin Riego, personal interview, November 22, 2016
3. Fr Armand Puig, personal interview, November 2014
4. Marisa Jimenez Buedo, personal interview, October 2015
5. Jorge Rodriguez, personal interview, April 2018
6. José María Blázquez Martínez, pp. 176-179
7. Dr. Andreu Muñoz; personal interview notes—pg. 2, March 2016
8. Instituto Vida Romana de Tarraco: http://institutviladomat.cat/portfoli/15analopez/2018/05/07/visita-per-tarragona/ downloaded on Nov. 12 2018
9. Spain Tourism Bureau, "Treasures of Tarragona," retrieved 8/12/2016, https://www.spain.info/en_US/reportajes/los_tesoros_romanos_de_tarragona.html
10. Dr. Andreu Muñoz, The Director of the Biblical Museum of Tarragona, gives an amazing account of how the ruins below the Cathedral provide evidence of the Temple of Augusto having been built there.
11. J.D. Douglas, Zondervan Illustrated Bible Dictionary, pp. 1388
12. Catholic Encyclopedia, James The Greater, downloaded on 11/25/2017 http://www.newadvent.org/cathen/08279b.htm
13. "Message to Kings" Podcast https://www.podomatic.com/podcasts/messagetokings/episodes/2016-01-15T20_39_59-08_00
14. Phoenicia.org website, fifth paragraph https://phoenicia.org/colonies.html Jan 14, 2019
15. Map obtained from Sutori online in their History of Oceanography section, retrieved Aug. 17, 2019 https://www.sutori.com/item/1500-bc-the-phoenicians-become-the-premier-shipbuilders-sailors-and-traders-t

16 http://christinprophecy.org/articles/the-dispersion-of-the-jews/
17 History of the Jews in Spain, http://kehillatisrael.net/docs/learning/sephardim.html, fourth paragraph, retrieved 3/30/2016
18 Ibid, sixth paragraph
19 Manuel Sotomayor, Vol 1, p. 81
20 Ibid, p. 81
21 Ibid, p. 82
22 Ibid, p. 82
23 Note, this point is made after having had conversations with F. Armand Puig, Dean of the Theological Institute of Catalunya, who provided a summary of the proceedings of the conference held in 2008 in Tarragona on Paul having conducted a missionary trip to Hispania. He mentioned the conclusion of several researchers, including the highly respected biblical historian and expert on the Apostle Paul, Murphy-O'connor. Murphy-O'Connor made this point in his book listed in the bibliography section of this book on p. 220
24 Kenneth Berding,
25 Jerome Murphy-O'Connor, p.221
26 Fr. Serafin de Ausejo, "San Pablo en España," *Revista Institucional de la Universidad de Sevilla*, retrieved July 2010 http://institucional.us.es/revistas/rasbl/5/art_7.pdf
27 Zenit.org, "International Conference, Pablo, Fructuoso, and Early Christianity", held in Tarragona, July 8, 2008
28 *Acts of Peter*, Ch. III, first paragraph
29 Murhy-O'Connor, p. 220
30 Probe Ministries; *The Historical Reliability of the Gospels*, August 2009, downloaded on 12/26/2017 https://bible.org/article/historical-reliability-gospels
31 CARRERAS MONFORT C. A new perspective for the demographic study of Roman Spain. *Revista de Historia da Arte eArqueologia n.2*, 1995-1996; pp. 69.
32 This image shows Paul speaking to the Jewish leaders; taken from http://biblescripture.net/Acts.html
33 Sotomayor, M; p. 160
34 Note: the reference to this map was taken from the "Commons" references of Wikimedia, so it is not totally authenticated. That said, it does generally match all the other documentation that exists on the existence of Roman Empire communities and that the Baetica region was one of the most intensely populated. The fact it was a Senatorial Province itself and the only one in Hispania or in other nearby regions of the Empire would corroborate

this point. There are also a number of other documented writings that point to the fact the northwestern area of the Tarraconensis Province was very scarcely populated. This reference was downloaded from Wikimedia on 2/5/17 and attributed to Cresthaven, https://commons.wikimedia.org/w/index.php?curid=38199606,

35 Sotomayor, Op cit., M; p. 161
36 Sotomayor, Op cit., M; p. 162
37 Image below taken from http://gardenofpraise.com/bibl75s.htm : Paul speaks to visitors in Rome
38 This conclusion is based on a number of historical documents, including Eusebius' *Ecclesiastical History of the Church*, written in the year 325 AD.
39 Sotomayor, p.82
40 Puig, 2015 personal interview
41 Murphy O'Connor, p 221
42 http://www.catholictradition.org/Tradition/saint-paul.htm ; www.goodsalt.com, retrieved January 21, 2018
43 Munoz, A; March 2016
44 Murphy O'Connor, p 221
45 https://en.wikipedia.org/wiki/Pope_Clement_I Picture downloaded December 12, 2016
46 John Chapman, *New Advent Catholic Encyclopedia Online*
47 W.C Van Unnik, p. 118.
48 The Didache, http://www.newadvent.org/cathen/04779a.htm , Catholic Encyclopedia
49 Joseph Barber, p.274.
50 The term "Apostolic Father of the Church" is the reference to those church leaders who were personal witnesses to one of the Apostles or of Paul. This is to differentiate from future church leaders who have also been designated as "Fathers of the Church."
51 J. Wood, p. 26
52 Dario Fernandez-Morera, pp. 281-82.
53 Catholic Encyclopedia, Obtained from the Internet, 12/27/2015: http://www.newadvent.org/cathen/02605b.htm
54 Muratori, pp 809–880
55 Ibid; Picture taken from above report
56 Ibid, p. 854
57 Geoffrey Mark Hahneman, "The Muratorian Fragment and the Development of the Canon." (Oxford: Clarendon) 1992. Sundberg, Albert C., Jr. "Canon

Muratori: A Fourth Century List" in *Harvard Theological Review* 66 (1973): 1–41.

58 M.R James, *The Apocryphal New Testament, Translations and Notes*, "Acts of Peter, III, the Vercelli Acts", Passage I; first paragraph. Oxford, Clarendon Press, 1924; http://www.earlychristianwritings.com/text/actspeter.html

59 International Standard Bible Encyclopedia

60 Lee Martin McDonald, (2009). *Forgotten Scriptures: The Selection and Rejection of Early Religious Writings*. Louisville, KY 40202-1396. pp. 11–33. ISBN 978-0664233570. Retrieved 24 November 2015.

61 *New Catholic Encyclopedia*, "Council of Trent"

62 Sotomayor, op.cit. page 163

63 EarlyChristianWrigings.com http://www.earlychristianwritings.com/text/actspeter.html "Vercelli Acts," Passage I retrieved Jan. 24, 2018,

64 M.R.James, Passage I; first paragraph.

65 Ibid, second paragraph

66 Picture taken from https://en.wikipedia.org/wiki/Athanasius_of_Alexandria downloaded Dec. 12, 2016

67 Sotomayor, Op cit., pg 164

68 Samuel Macauley Jackson, ed., "Cyril of Jersusalem", *New Schaff-Herzog Encyclopedia of Religious Knowledge*, (3rd ed.) p.334, London and New York, Funk & Wagnalls, 1914

69 Picture taken from: http://www.orthodoxchurchquotes.com/category/sayings-from-saints-elders-and-fathers/st-cyril-of-jerusalem/ Downloaded December 12, 2016

70 Sotomayor, Op cit., page 164

71 Ibid,164

72 See Wilken, p. xv, and also "John Chrysostom" in *Encyclopaedia Judaica*; Wilken, Robert Louis (1983). *John Chrysostom and the Jews: Rhetoric and Reality in the Late Fourth Century*. Berkeley: University of California Press.

73 Sotomayor, op. cit. page 163

74 Ibid, page 163

75 Enrique Flores, España Sagrada, Paulus in Hispaniam, page 49

76 Image taken from http://www.newadvent.org/cathen/14574b.htm

77 Sotomayor, op. cit., pg. 164

78 Photo obtained from the Ecija Board of Tourism

79 Catholic Encyclopedia

80 Image taken from: http://www.catholic.org/saints/saint.php?saint_id=652 Downloaded Dec. 12, 2016

81. Sotomayor, op.cit., pg. 164
82. Murphy-O'Connor, p. 44
83. Annuario Pontificio 2012, pp. 3-8
84. Some historians have Clement I as the fourth Bishop of Rome (Pope) following Peter, Linus, and Cletus, while others have him as third following Linus.
85. Demetrius Kiminas, p. 16.
86. Puig, personal interview, November 2014
87. Sotomayor, op. cit, p. 89
88. Purificacion Urbina, personal interview, November 2014
89. Juan Jose Ayan, et. al; *Osio de Cordoba*, Editorial Biblioteca de Autores Cristianos, Madrid, pg. 23
90. Sotomayor, op. cit. p.90
91. As mentioned on this page, the exact year in which the Council was held is of considerable controversy, and much has been written about this. An analysis of a few of the proceedings indicate a date of the year 324 and therefore some writers have assigned that year as to the date of the Council. This conclusion, however, does not consider that a couple of other Councils that followed it between the years 310 and 325 made reference to Elvira having already taken place. Others have suggested the years 305, 309 and 313, but these have not considered the brutal persecution launched by one of the Tetrarchy Emperors, Diocletian, in 304 that lasted around 10 years. The Roman Empire had been divided into four regions, and Diocletian convinced the other three emperors to launch such a persecution of Christians. In Hispania, under Emperor Maximian, the persecutions were not as intense during those ten years. It would be illogical, however, to consider a Council with such a large gathering of Christians coming together in a public forum during the time that there was an open edict of persecutions by the Tetrarchy Emperors. That is why many current biblical historians are now suggesting the years 300 to 304, which was just prior to the Diocletian persecution.
92. Map downloaded from https://commons.wikimedia.org/wiki/File:Tetrarchy_map3.jpg
93. Timothy Barnes, *Constantine and Eusebius*, 41–42;
94. Eusebius of Caesarea, *Life of Constantine*.
95. Eusebius of Caesarea, and other Biblical sources, have documented that Constantine experienced his conversion in 312 at the Battle of the Milvian Bridge after which Constantine claimed the Emperorship for the Western Roman Empire. According to numerous sources, Constantine looked to the sky before the battle and saw a cross, and with it the Greek words "In this sign, you will conquer." Constantine then commanded his troops to place the

sign of the cross on each shield, and eventually they were victorious in the battle. Constantine believed that it was the power of God and the Christian symbol of the Cross that led his troops to victory.

96 Francis Mersham, "St. Vincent" pg. 1912, in New Advent Catholic Encyclopedia

97 Sotomayor, Op. cit, pp. 164

98 New Advent Catholic Encyclopedia, Definition of an Ecclesiastical Council; Ecclesiastical (or Ecumenical) Councils are legally convened assemblies of ecclesiastical dignitaries and theological experts for the purpose of discussing and regulating matters of church doctrine and discipline, also known as "canons." http://www.newadvent.org/cathen/04423f.htm ; downloaded January 6, 2016

99 New Advent Catholic Encyclopedia, "Council of Nicaea," http://www.newadvent.org/cathen/11044a.htm ; downloaded January 6, 2016

100 Ibid

101 Ayan, Op. Cit., page 35

102 Sotomayor, Op. Cit., p. 64

103 Patrick Wall, "Canons of Elvira," Awrsipe.com. 1,2017. http://www.awrsipe.com/patrick_wall/selected_documents/309%20Council%20of%20Elvira.pdf Accessed July

104 Image shows Emperor Constantine is in the middle and reportedly, Bishop Osio of Cordoba (Hispania) is to his right; Downloaded December 12, 2016 https://en.wikipedia.org/wiki/Nicene_Creed

105 William B Maltby,. "The Black Legend" in *Encyclopedia of Latin American History and Culture*, vol. 1, pp. 346-348. New York: Charles Scribner's Sons 1996.

106 Braulio Rodriguez Plaza, "Conferencia sobre Isabel la Catolica y la Evangelizacion de America," Encuentro ante los embajadores de Hispanoamerica, 12 de noviembre del 20013

107 Zenit, Christian Online Publications, Editorial, May 4, 2003, downloaded https://es.zenit.org/articles/el-papa-se-despide-hasta-siempre-espana-hasta-siempre-tierra-de-maria/ August 15, 2018

108 David Green, Columnist for the Haaretz—Jewish History; http://www.haaretz.com/jewish/this-day-in-jewish-history/1.684854, Retrieved on January 10, 2017

109 Map taken from: https://commons.wikimedia.org/wiki/File:Hispania_586_AD.PNG Wikimedia Commons, which allow for documents from the public domain to be used with no copyright restrictions

110 Roger Collins, p.44

111 Map taken from Wikimedia Commons, documenting there are no copyright violations https://commons.wikimedia.org/wiki/File:Map_of_expansion_of_Caliphate.svg

112 Encyclopedia Britannica Online: https://www.britannica.com/topic/Umayyad-dynasty-Islamic-history ; downloaded on July 30, 2016

113 Hispanic Muslims, http://www.hispanicmuslims.com/andalusia/andalusia.html Accessed from website on March 20, 2018

114 Encyclopedia Britannica, Opcit,

115 Image taken from Google Images, downloaded July 30,2016

116 Ibid

117 Catholic News Agency, http://www.catholicnewsagency.com/cw/post.php?id=676 downloaded 3/23/2017

118 Isabel Allardyce, Historic Shrines of Spain, Franciscan Missionary Press, New York, 1912, p. 33

119 Map taken from the Historical Maps of the Mediterranean, http://explorethemed.com/reconquista.asp

120 Jewish Wikipedia, Muslim Invasion and the Reconquista http://www.jewishwikipedia.info/musliminvasion.html

121 Euratlas, Kingdom of the Almoravids, retrieved 8/5/2017 https://www.euratlas.net/history/europe/1100/entity_3242.html

122 Colegios Sagrado Corazon blogspot, *Mediaval Spain*, http://medievalspain5thprimary.blogspot.com/2017/05/iii-christian-kingdoms-3.html, downloaded May 10, 2018

123 Image from: http://catholicsaints.info/saint-ferdinand-iii-of-castille/

124 Braulio Rodriguez Plaza, Conference speech November 2003

125 William Maltby, Op.cit., p. 346

126 Raymond Dacey, pp. 563-574

127 *Bible Archeology*, "New Discoveries Relating to the Apostle Paul," http://www.biblearchaeology.org/post/2009/10/08/New-Discoveries-Relating-to-the-Apostle-Paul.aspx retrieved on 12/29/2016

128 Map obtained from the Internet, http://historylink101.com/2/Rome/roman-ships.htm retrieved 1/5/2018

129 Muñoz, op. cit., personal interview

130 Illustration obtained from the archives of the Biblical Museum of Tarragona, November, 2017

131 Antonio de Quintanadueñas, *Santos de la Ciudad de Sevilla*,

132 Blue Letter Bible, "Paul's Travel Timeline", retrieved May 3, 2018 https://www.blueletterbible.org/study/paul/timeline.cfm

133 This image shows Paul speaking to the Jewish leaders; taken from http://biblescripture.net/Acts.html

134 Temple Mount.Org http://www.templemount.org/destruct2.html; accessed on Sept. 29, 2016

135 Jewish Virtual Library, "Moises-Maimonides-Rambam," retrieved March 2017 http://www.jewishvirtuallibrary.org/moses-maimonides-rambam

136 Downloaded from Wikipedia on March 7, 2018, https://en.wikipedia.org/wiki/Mishneh_Torah

137 Britannica Online, "Mishne Torah" retrieved on March 7, 2018 https://www.britannica.com/topic/Mishne-Torah

138 Sacred Text Archives Accessed, "Talmud," retrieved February 17, 2018 http://www.sacred-texts.com/jud/talmud.htm

139 J.B De Long, p. 678

140 UNESCO World Heritage Site, http://whc.unesco.org/en/list/313 downloaded on December 22, 2014

141 Liz Sonneborn, p.31

142 Ibid, p. 89

143 A Chejne, *Muslim Spain—Its History and Culture*

BIBLIOGRAPHY

Note: This continues to be work in progress with additional sources that are being found on a continuing basis that will be included in future editions of this book

Allardyce, Isabel. *Historic Shrines of Spain*, Franciscan Missionary Press, New York, 1912, p. 33

Annuario Pontificio. 2012 Edition (this is the annual directory of the Catholic Church's Holy See that lists all Popes, Cardinals, and Bishops from around the world since early Christianity, as well as departments and diplomatic missions). Retrieved on July 7, 2017.

Ayan, Juan Jose; Manuel Crespo, Pilar Gonzalez, Jesus Polo, *Osio de Cordoba*, Editorial Biblioteca de Autores Cristianos, Madrid, Spain, 2013 ISBN:9788422016489

Barber, Joseph; "The First Epistle of Clement to the Corinthians, 5:5–6", translated by J.B. Lightfoot,. *The Apostolic Fathers: A Revised Text with Introductions, Notes, Dissertations, and Translations, St. Clement of Rome; London: MacMillan and Co. 1869.*

Barnes, Timothy D., *Constantine and Eusebius*. Cambridge, MA: Harvard University Press, 1981. ISBN 978-0-674-16531-1

Beltrán, D. Antonio; *El Santo Cáliz de la Catedral de Valencia* (Imprenta Nacher, Valencia 1984, 2ª edición)

Berding, Kenneth, "Biblical Exposition, New Testament Historical Theology", The Good Book Blog, http://www.thegoodbookblog.com/2015/apr/14/pauls-4th-missionary-journey-and-i-dont-mean-his-t/ Retrieved April 14, 2015

Blázquez Martínez, José María; *Notas a la contribución de la Península Ibérica al erario de la República romana*, [Publicado previamente en: *Homenagem ao Prof. Doutor Mendes Correa (Trabalhos da sociedade portuguesa de Antropologia e Etnologia* 16), Porto 1959.

Cathedral of Santiago website; http://www.catedraldesantiago.es/en/node/467 , information retrieved on August 15, 2016

Catholic Encyclopedia; multiple references used; http://www.newadvent.org/cathen/a.htm

Cathedral of Valencia; Online website: http://www.catedraldevalencia.es/en/

Catholic News Agency, http://www.catholicnewsagency.com/blog/all-of-your-burning-questions-on-holy-years-and-doors-answered/ Retrieved on July 10, 2016

Chapman, John; "Pope St. Clement I", in *New Advent Catholic Encyclopedia*; 1908

Chejne, A., *Muslim Spain—Its History and Culture*, The university of Minnesota Press, Minneapolis, 1974.

Collins, Roger. *Visigothic Spain, 409–711*. Oxford: Blackwell Publishing, 2004.

Dacey, Raymond; "A Theory of Conclusions," *Philosophy of Science*, Vol. 45, No. 4; pp. 563-574; The University of Chicago Press; Dec., 1978.

De Aseo, Fr. Serafín. San Pablo: Misionero en España y Particularmente en la Bética. Revista Institucional Universidad de Sevilla. Retrieved July, 2010 http://institucional.us.es/revistas/rasbl/5/art_7.pdf

De Long, J. B. and Shleifer, A.; "Princes and Merchants: European City Growth Before the Industrial Revolution;" *The Journal of Law and Economics*, University of Chicago Press, 36 (2): 671-678 , October 1993

Douglas, J. D., Tenney, Merrill C.; Zondervan *Illustrated Bible Dictionary*; Zondervan, Grand Rapids, Michigan, 2009

EarlyChristianWritings.com entire version of Acts of Peter: http://www.earlychristianwritings.com/text/actspeter.html retrieved January 2018

Encyclopedia Britannica Online: https://www.britannica.com/topic/Umayyad-dynasty-Islamic-history; downloaded on July 30, 2016

Eusebius of Caesera, *Life of Constantine*, reprinted by Clarendon Press, Sept. 9, 1999

Eusebius of Caesera, *Ecclesiatical History,* 313 AD

Euratlas, Online Atlas resource for Europe history and geography https://www.euratlas.net/history/europe/aegean/index.html

Fernandez-Morera, Dario; "Cronica del Moro Rasis" in: *The Myth of the Andalusian Paradise: Muslims, Christians, and Jews under Islamic Rule in Medieval Spain,* Publisher ISI Books, University of Chicago Press, 2016

Fernandez Urbiña, Jose; Professor and historians from the University of Granada, who provided insights into the importance of the Council of Elvira and of Paul's visit to Hispania.

Frier, Bruce W. "Demography", in Alan K. Bowman, Peter Garnsey, and Dominic Rathbone, eds., *The Cambridge Ancient History XI: The High Empire, A.D. 70–192,* (Cambridge: Cambridge University Press, 2000), pp. 810–54. https://archive.org/stream/iB_Ca/011_djvu.txt Downloaded Aug. 15, 2018

Green, David; Columnist for the Haaretz—Jewish History; downloaded on January 10, 2017; http://www.haaretz.com/jewish/this-day-in-jewish-history/1.684854

Hahneman, Geoffrey Mark. *The Muratorian Fragment and the Development of the Canon.* (Oxford: Clarendon) 1992. Sundberg, Albert C., Jr. "Canon Muratori: A Fourth Century List" in *Harvard Theological Review* 66 (1973): 1–41. Obtained from the Internet on 12/27/2015

International Standard Bible Encyclopedia, *The Apocryphal Gospels,* www.biblestudytools.com retrieved July 2017

Jimenez Buedo, Marisa; Director Archbishop of Tarragona, personal interviews October 2015 and November 2016

Kiminas, Demetrius (2009). *The Ecumenical Patriarchate.* First Edition, Wildside Press. USA, 2009

Lindemann, Andreas. "The First Epistle of Clement." In *The Apostolic Fathers: An Introduction.* Edited by Wilhelm Pratscher, 47–69. Waco, TX: Baylor University Press, 2010.

Loring, P., Jorge: El Santo Grial (Caliz de Jesus) https://www.youtube.com/watch?v=gyb9UTWBYDw

Malka, Jeff; Who are the Sephardim—A Brief History, Sphardic Geneology Resources, http://www.jewishgen.org/Sephardic/SEPH_who.HTM; downloaded, January 21, 2017

Maltby, William B. "The Black Legend" in *Encyclopedia of Latin American History and Culture*, vol. 1, pp. 346-348. New York: Charles Scribner's Sons 1996.

Manfredi, Juan Luis; Chair and professor of Journalism and Communications at the University of Seville, Spain, who provided insights into Catholicism in Spain

Martín Riego, P. Manuel; Church Historian, Director and Editor of the Center for Theological Studies of Seville. Several personal interviews were conducted with him at his home city of Seville during 2016 and 2017.

McDonald, Lee Martin (2009). Forgotten Scriptures: The Selection and Rejection of Early Religious Writings. Louisville, KY 40202-1396. pp. 11–33. ISBN 978-0664233570. Retrieved 24 November 2015.

Mershman, Francis. "*St. Vincent*" in the Catholic Encyclopedia, Vol. 15., New York, Robert Appleton Company publishers, 1912, Vol. 15, 2015: Mershman, Francis. "St. Vincent." The Catholic Encyclopedia. Vol. 15. New York: Robert Appleton Company, 1912. 12 Feb. 2015

Muratori, *Antiquitates Italicae Medii Aevii* (Milan 1740), vol. III, pp 809–880. Located within *Dissertatio XLIII* ; English Translation from Bruce M. Metzger, obtained from Early Christian Writings website, downloaded on 5/6/2017 http://www.earlychristianwritings.com/muratorian.html .

Muñoz, Andreu; Director of the Biblical Museum of Tarragona; references based on several personal interviews with Fernando Figueredo, conducted multiple times between 2015-2017.

Murphy-O'Connor, Jerome; *Paul History*, Oxford University Press, Oxford, England, 2012

Murphy-O'Connor, *Paul a Critical Life*, Oxford Clarendon Press, 1996;

National Geographic documentary; Holy Grail Endures; Downloaded March 12, 2013 http://science.nationalgeographic.com/science/archaeology/holy-grail/

New Catholic Encyclopedia (Vol. 3 ed.). , Washington, DC 20064: Catholic University of America. 2003. pp. 20, 26.

Puig, Armand. Dean of the Theological Institute of Catalonia. Notes from personal interview with Fernando Figueredo conducted multiple times in 2015 and 2016.

Pujol, Jaime, Archbishop of Diocese of Tarragona. Notes from personal interview with Fernando Figueredo conduct in March 2015.

Quintanadueñas, Antonio de. *Santos de la Ciudad de Sevilla*. Publisher Francisco de Lyra, Sevilla 1637

Rodríguez, Jorge-Manuel, President, Sindonology Center of Spain, Personal Interview, April 19, 2018

Rodriguez Plaza, Braulio—Arzobispo de Toledo, *Conferencia sobre Isabel la Catolica y la Evangelizacion de America,* Encuentro ante los embajadores de Hispanoamerica, 12 de noviembre del 20013

Sonneborn, Liz (2006). *Averroes (Ibn Rushd): Muslim Scholar, Philosopher, and Physician of the Twelfth Century*. The Rosen Publishing Group., ISBN 1404205144. Retrieved November 3, 2012.

Sotomayor-Muro, M; Gonzalez, T; Lopez, P; *Historia de la Iglesia en Espana (History of the Church in Spain);* Biblioteca de Autores Cristianos Publisher, Madrid, 1979

Ubric Rabaneda, Purificación; Professor and archeologist from the University of Granada, who provided insights into the importance of the Council of Elvira.

Van Unnik, W.C. "Studies on the so-called First Epistle of Clement. The literary genre," in Cilliers Breytenbach and Laurence L. Welborn, *Encounters with Hellenism: Studies on the First Letter of Clement,* Leiden & Boston: Brill, 2004, p. 118.

Vanguardia News, *Historiadores de Acuerdo que Pablo viajo a Tarragona*; http://www.lavanguardia.es/lv24h/200...485325044.html

Vatican City. "What is a Holy Year?". 17 February, 1997. Accessed on October 2, 2016 http://www.vatican.va/jubilee_2000/docs/documents/ju_documents_17-feb-1997_history_en.html

Vatican City. "Biblioteca Apostolica Vaticana." Caps. I, fasc. 1, n. 8; https://www.facsimilefinder.com/facsimiles/bull-first-jubilee-christianity-boniface-viii-facsimile

Wall, Patrick. "Canons of Elvira". Awrsipe.com. Accessed July 1,2017. http://www.awrsipe.com/patrick_wall/selected_documents/309%20Council%20of%20Elvira.pdf

WikiMedia Commons; Provides works into the public domain to avoid copyright violations, https://commons.wikimedia.org/wiki/File:Hispania_586_AD.PNG

Wood, Jamie. "Brill's Series on the Middel Ages—21" in *The Politics of Identity in Visigothic Spain: Religion and Power in the Histories of Isidore of Seville*. Online

Book Laiden and Boston: BRILL. pp. 26–. ISBN 978-90-04-20990-9. Retrieved July 21, 2017.

Zenit.org, "International Conference, Pablo, Fructuoso, and Early Christianity", held in Tarragona, July 8, 2008

ABOUT THE AUTHOR

DR. FERNANDO FIGUEREDO is a distinguished and highly respected professional with extensive experience in academia, corporate communications and international travel. His personal passion for years has been the early history of Christianity, which led him to establish History Travel Tours (HTT), a company that conducts tours and pilgrimages focused on historical elements and early Christianity.

While completing his doctoral studies at the University of Seville in Spain, Dr. Figueredo became intrigued with the amazing history of Spain, which goes back over 5,000 years. In particular, he became very interested in the period of time when Spain was under Roman rule, from the years 200-BC to 400-AD.

Known at the time as Hispania, Christianity flourished in Hispania to a very advanced level by the year 300 AD, with a number of historical facts that position this region of the then Roman Empire as being critically important in the evolution of early Christian tenets, beliefs, and norms.

It all started when in Seville, finishing his doctoral studies, Dr. Figueredo's wife planned a last minute, short weekend trip to the nearby city of Ecija, between Seville and Cordoba. To their surprise, in his homily the priest mentioned the missionary trip to Ecija by the Apostle Paul during his trip to Hispania, back between the years 64-66 AD. Dr. Figueredo and his wife were both stunned by the mention of St. Paul having been in Hispania since both were devout Catholics and very knowledgeable of early Christian history.

Dr. Figueredo then became intrigued with the possibility of Paul having been in Hispania and that launched a ten-year research project that has led the writing of this book.

It should be noted that Dr. Figueredo has had a very successful career in Academia as well as Corporate Communications. He most recently held a series of important executive administrative as well as teaching positions at Florida International University (FIU), the fourth largest university in student enrollment in 2019, with around 60,000 students. Ranked as a top-100 public university in the U.S., FIU is also ranked No.1 in students of Hispanic heritage with 65% of the student body with such heritage, and top-10 in total minorities. FIU also has a large international faculty and student body, representing over 135 countries.

Dr. Figueredo's professional career advanced through an increasingly important number of corporate positions after graduation from the University of Florida with a BS in Industrial Engineering. He rose to a position as Region Director of Corporate and External Affairs with Bell South-Florida, then to a Region Director of Consumer Communications for AT&T Latin America. He was then named Vice President of Corporate Communications for Lucent Technologies Latin America, when Lucent was divested from AT&T. He later became a partner in a top-5 Global Public Relations firm, Porter Novelli. Because Dr. Figueredo was highly respected as a communications professional, who was also considered to have no "political baggage," he was chosen in 2011 by the then Mayor of Miami Dade County to serve as the Director of Communications and External Affairs for Miami-Dade County, a position he held with distinction for three years.

Dr. Figueredo holds a Ph.D. in Mass Communications from the University of Seville in Spain. He also holds a master's degree in business administration from Florida International University with emphasis on marketing communications and a BS degree in industrial engineering from the University of Florida. He has attended numerous senior level management seminars at prestigious institutions such as The London Business School, Babson University, Georgetown University, and the University of Pennsylvania.

Made in the USA
Las Vegas, NV
16 April 2023